Creative Design
in Bobbin Lace

He who works with his hands is a labourer.
He who works with his hands and his head is a
craftsman.
He who works with his hands and his head and
his heart is an artist.

St Francis of Assisi

Creative Design in Bobbin Lace

Ann Collier

B.T. BATSFORD Ltd, LONDON

956244 01 1

First published 1982
© Ann Collier 1982

ISBN 0 7134 2393 5

Filmset in Monophoto Plantin by
Servis Filmsetting Ltd, Manchester

Printed in Great Britain by The Anchor Press Ltd
Tiptree Essex
for the publishers,
B.T. Batsford Ltd,
4 Fitzhardinge Street, London W1H 0AH

Contents

Colour Photographs

Acknowledgements

A large proportion of the lace in this book has been designed and worked by myself and some of the antique lace is from my own collection, but I would like to thank the English Lace School, The Victoria and Albert Museum, The Cecil Higgins Art Gallery, The Kantcentrum in Bruges and Initiation à la Dentelle in Le Puy for allowing me to show some of their pieces.

The photos in figs 27, 70, 71, 75, 76 and 77 were taken by Pavel Janek.

My thanks also to the many people from Britain, the Continent and America for their co-operation, to my students who have tried out designs, to my mother for checking the text and to my husband for all his work on the photography.

The History and Development of Technique

Bobbin lace is a form of weaving, but instead of a close-woven texture ways have been developed to form open areas merely by the different movements of the bobbins and arrangement of the pins. Each thread in the construction can move independently on its bobbin, unlike the rigid warp threads of a loom.

Bobbin lace began in two different areas in Europe. In Belgium the Flemish workers evolved a tape-like form of lace with different combinations of stitch to form looser or tighter weaves. This tape narrowed or widened to produce a recognisable shape. The Isabella and Albrecht quilt, made in Brussels in 1599, is interpreted in this way with various saints and kings depicted. The whole seems to have been worked from cartoon drawings.

In Italy, near Genoa, lace was made in plaited form, copying the needle laces of the period.

The early tape form was developed further in both countries and it was often decorated by the inclusion of holes and picots. It was formed into a scrolling pattern with open areas; these were filled afterwards with a net

mesh. This type of lace is referred to as Flemish or Milanese. (Fig. 1)

Lace construction then began to divide into two distinct groups, particularly when flax could be more finely spun. Lace was found to im-

Fig. 1 Flemish lace in braid form, increasing and decreasing in size and decorated with holes, with the background added afterwards

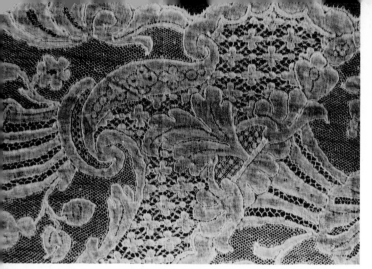

Fig. 2 Part of a Mechlin lappet; one piece lace with a high proportion of cloth work sometimes decorated with holes and twists. Gimp thread emphasises the design and separates it from the wide variety of fillings

Fig. 3 Valenciennes with a flowing carnation design worked in one piece, but with the dense ground it required no gimp thread

prove when background and design were worked simultaneously; there were fewer knots and loose threads, making the lace reversible. This technique required a large number of bobbins and consequently took longer to make. Various districts in Belgium developed their individual lace styles – Mechlin or Malines, Valenciennes and Binche.

Malines had a soft shiny thread to outline the design and make it stand out; light and shade were created by the different stitches that were used in the fillings. Numerous combinations of stitch and the fine thread produced a lace of great beauty and artistic merit. (Fig. 2)

Valenciennes had a very dense background which changed later to a plaited mesh. This gave a large number of threads for use in the main design which is flat and closely-woven, requiring no other thread to outline it. (Fig. 3)

Binche made more use of the complicated filling stitches and the pattern was formed with these rather than by areas of woven cloth stitch. (Fig. 4)

The relationship between solid area and mesh is more apparent in the one-piece laces. If the mesh is close there are more threads available for the cloth stitch pattern. If a more open net is used the cloth stitch areas are rather thin and starved, and therefore need a heavier thread, called a gimp, to outline the design.

In the Brussels area further development was made in the tape motif method of construction. Using the fine linen thread the individual motifs of the design were worked first, the loose threads moving in rope form from area to area as the design progressed. On leaves and flowers the roping formed a raised edge which,

Fig. 4 Binche, or Point de Fée, showing the elaborate use of stitches

Fig. 5 Detail of lady from the panel in Fig. 45 made in Brussels motif form, with raised edges which gave dimension as well as carrying threads from one part of the design to another. Mainly cloth or half stitch with very little use of filling

incorporated into the design, gave dimension. When the main body of the design was complete the bobbins were linked in again and background and fillings worked, tying them off or carrying them across the back of the work. The work was carried out on the wrong side for this reason and the finished lace was not reversible. It had the advantage that several workers could be employed on the same piece of lace, each using their own special skills. Some made the motifs, some worked the fillings and another group assembled them and joined them together with either bars or mesh.

Lacemaking spread to other parts of Europe and again districts gave their name to the style. In northern France, Chantilly and Lille were made. Both of these are one piece laces. Chantilly used a more open cloth in half stitch for the main part of the design, outlined in a heavy gimp, and the background used a light twisted net. Lille used the more dense cloth stitch surrounded by gimp and the same net.

Blonde lace was so named because of the cream silk that was used in its

9

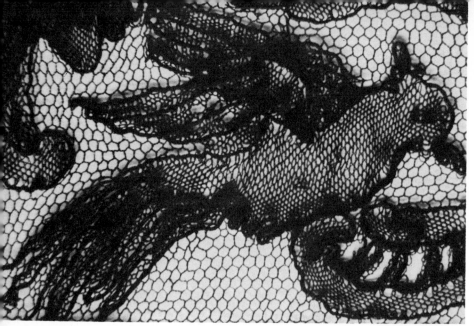

Fig. 6 Bird in Chantilly from Fig. 47 showing the use of half stitch and gimp threads for the main design and the fine twisted net as background

Fig. 7 BELOW Blonde lace with a heavy silk thread used for weavers on the solid cloth stitch areas and for the gimp thread. Fine silk thread used in contrast for the shaded areas in half stitch and for the twisted net background. Extensive use of large honeycomb holes to give a third shading

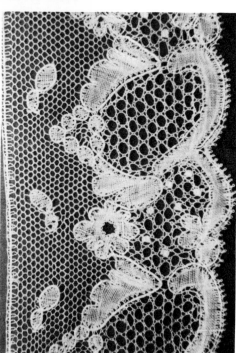

Fig. 8 ABOVE English Point ground, probably from Buckinghamshire, with twisted net, honeycomb fillings, use of tallies and with a cloth stitch pattern surrounded with gimp. The gimp thread is used as continuously as was possible

Fig. 9 Part of a Honiton Shawl which shows the use of fillings, picot stems and raised or rolled edges

construction. It was made in all areas and is characterised by its dense pattern and light ground, achieved by using a thicker thread for the pattern and a lighter one for the ground. This enabled the workers to obtain much more contrast between light and shade. (Fig. 7)

Refugees from the religious persecutions in Europe fled to Britain and brought with them the art of bobbin lace making. Those from France settled in the Midlands, Northampton, Buckinghamshire and Bedfordshire and introduced Lille-type one piece lace. Belgians came to South Devon where the motif-type lace was introduced and developed into Honiton, again named after the area. Honiton developed a wide variety of filling stitches, very different to the Belgian ones and this, combined with its naturalistic design, gave it its distinct character. (Fig. 9)

Although large quantities of lace were being made, it was too expensive for any but the wealthy and was treasured by each generation. It was worn by both men and women until the Victorian era, when men changed to a more austere mode of dress.

With the advent of the Industrial Revolution machine-made net appeared. Motifs from Brussels and Honiton were sewn onto it as background, making it quicker and

easier to produce, and it was not to be long before the machine could make most of the laces formerly made by hand. The designs were based on the old prickings. Machine lace became both cheap and plentiful and was indistinguishable from the hand made. The only way to compete was to make it by a faster method and to try to produce designs that the machine could not copy.

The old plaited laces of Genoa, housed in the Cluny Museum in Paris, were copied in a coarser thread and a bolder pattern, and thus the process was quickened. The background consisted of plaited bars instead of net and various petal and leaf formations made it easier to work than the old point ground. It was developed in Malta, Bedfordshire and Le Puy and in its early days some fine design and workmanship was produced. Speed, however, led to poor quality and it did not compare to the fine lace of former years. Soon the machine could produce any style of lace and it was available to the masses. Hand made lace died as an industry and became just a hobby.

The wide variety of stitches, methods and techniques in bobbin lace have been evolved over many centuries by individual workers and in modern lace design we can use all of them to create the effect that we want.

TWO

Braid Lace

Equipment   Working bobbin lace

EQUIPMENT

Before one can begin to make lace, there are a few essentials necessary to the craft. One needs a surface on which to work, into which pins can be firmly inserted, bobbins on which thread can be wound and pins of a suitable size to support the thread used. One needs also to understand the principle of bobbin lace in order to produce satisfactory equipment.

Being a weaving craft, the construction threads are similar: warp threads are the passives and weft threads are the weavers. These weavers, as a pair, weave through the passive threads and are pinned firmly into place. The pattern is worked from a pricking or drawing, and the pins hold it level and taut. The passives, like the warp threads on a loom, need to be weighted in some way to keep the tension correct and the working surface must be firm enough to hold the pins throughout the working. Understanding this one can now plan the equipment.

Bobbins

Threads are wound on to bobbins to give them weight and to make manipulation easy. Traditionally, British bobbins had beads to give them extra weight while Continental ones had a bulbous piece at the bottom. The heavier the thread, the more weight is needed on the bobbin. The bobbins need to be of sufficient size to hold the amount of thread required to make the article, and the thread, though wound firmly, must run freely. Traditional shaped bobbins can be purchased both in wood and plastic but adequate ones can be made from doweling cut to size. They need a shank, a neck and a head as in diagram 1. The shank is held with the fingers; the neck holds the thread and the head prevents the thread coming off.

Pillow or Working Surface

Traditional pillows were stuffed with chopped straw, and though this method is still the best they can be made with horsehair, wood wool or with built up layers of carpet underlay (wool not foam). The important thing is that the surface must be very, very firm. Flat pieces of polystyrene can serve the purpose till they become pitted.

In order to keep the threads taut with the weight of the bobbins the pillow needs to be slightly domed so that the bobbins lie on a downhill slope, especially if working on the knee or table. A flat surface can only be used if worked upright or at an angle so that the bobbins hang down.

The shape or form that the pillow takes depends on how it is to be used and the size or shape of the piece to be worked. (Diagram 2). For small pieces that can be worked on the knee, a small round pillow is suitable; if working on

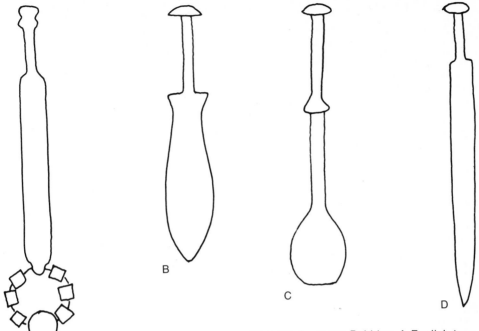

Diagram 1 ABOVE Bobbins. A English type with spangles, B Swedish, C Belgian, D Honiton

Diagram 2 BELOW Pillows. A Round cushion for Honiton, B Bolster for edges, C Revolving cylinder for edges, D Flemish type on a board base

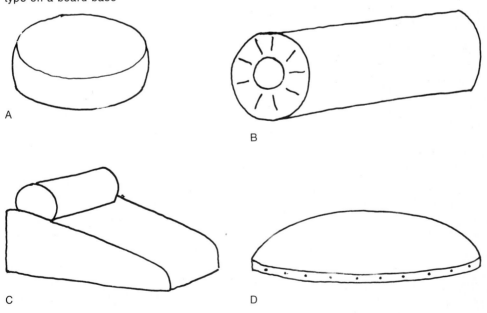

a table, a pillow on a board base is useful. A bolster shape needs support to stop it rolling but is useful for continuous patterns or large pieces of work, and a pillow with a revolving cylinder is useful for edges. When working on a wall hanging or other large items, a large piece of polystyrene from the packing round large household items suits the purpose well.

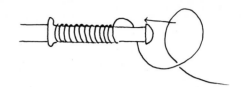

Diagram 3 Winding a bobbin and placing the half hitch by putting the loop on the bobbin head

To Make a Pillow on a Board Base
Requirements

A piece of plywood cut square or round, 46cm (18in) across.
A piece of firm material, 10cm (4in) bigger than the board all round.
Wool carpet felt.

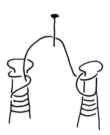

Diagram 4 Hanging a pair on a pin

Method

Cut two pieces of felt to the size of the board and three graduating in size. Place these on the board in order, the two large ones first, the smallest piece going on last. Cover with material and tack down to the under side of the board as tightly as possible.

Diagram 5 The first pattern worked out on graph paper

If straw is used, make a bag of material a little larger than the board and pack tightly with chopped straw. Cover with another piece of material and tack this to the underside as before. The pillow must be very firm and hard to touch.

WORKING BOBBIN LACE

When beginning bobbin lace it is necessary to have a pattern and the first one is made from graph paper as a guide to the spacing of the pins. Torchon and all net grounds are worked out on graph paper and the size of the paper depends on the size of thread to be used (see grids at the end of the book). Graph paper can be purchased in various sizes, at different angles and circular. Prick through the dots on the first pattern onto card and then pin the

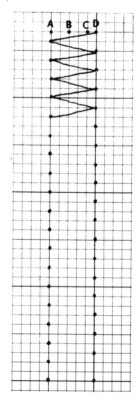

card to the pillow. Wind four pairs of bobbins, winding about 90cm (36in) on to one bobbin and then breaking off the same amount from the reel and winding this on to the second bobbin. Sylko 40 is suitable to begin with. Bobbins are always wound in pairs and the thread secured with a half hitch as shown; this holds the thread but allows it to run freely with the weight of the bobbin. Hang a pair on each pin A, B, C and D as in diagram 5.

The Basic Weaving or Cloth Stitch

Following the diagrams, begin on the right. Number the positions of the threads 1, 2, 3, 4 from the left. Move 2 across 3 to the right, then as one movement move the new 3 over 1 to the left and the new 4 over 3 to the left. Finally move the new 2 over 3 to the right. This complete movement is referred to as whole stitch, cloth stitch or linen stitch, and one can see that the weaving pair have moved through a pair to the left. Take these and the next pair to the left and number as before; repeat the stitch. Repeat this to the end of the row, cross the weaving pair twice right over left and pin into place. Now repeat the moves as before, weaving to the right but numbering the bobbins from the left. Continue to do this until it begins to become automatic.

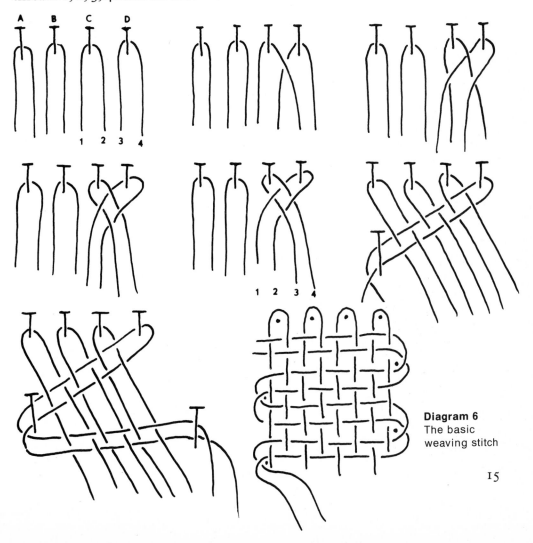

Diagram 6
The basic
weaving stitch

Adding a Foot

Hang another pair on to the pin in line with A and to the pin in line with D. Work across to the left but do not work through the new pair. Pin up the weavers as usual and then work through the new pair; twist the outside pair three times and the others once, then weave across to the right and repeat with the other new pair. Continue to do this, always pinning up the weavers before the last pair is reached and then working this edge stitch. A foot forms a straight edge to the tape; without it the braid has a loop like quality.

This tape can be varied in a number of ways. By twisting the weavers before and after every stitch, a vertical stripe will form. A similar effect is achieved by twisting the passives as well. Try a thicker pair introduced

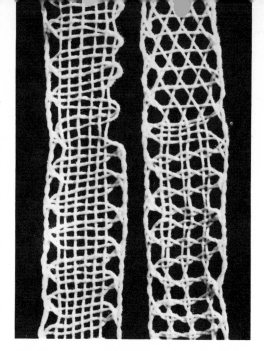

Fig. 10 Braid worked with and without a foot, in half stitch and with twists

into the centre of the braid to produce a raised effect. Experiment with the braid to see what effects can be obtained. Then cut off the threads, tie them, and then either rewind the bobbins or knot them together in pairs. Wind the knot away onto one of the bobbins, so that the knots do not appear all at once in the work.

Shaping the Braid

One of the easiest ways to design pieces of lace in motif form is with a shaped braid. This way of making lace is the basis of Brussels and Honiton lace. The Russians developed it further but its origin is in the Flemish schools.

The design is worked as a continuous braid. It must be made to curve and bend, and to join to itself where it touches to make a firm piece. The braid can be worked with or without a foot; this depends on personal preference and the effect required. A foot, however, does help the threads to stay in place on curves and bends.

To curve the braid there must be

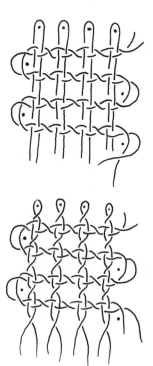

Diagram 7 Putting a twist into weavers or passives at every stitch

more pin holes on the outer edge than on the inner, and it is sometimes necessary to use a pin hole twice. Work through to the inner curve, pin up the weavers, and return with them to the outer edge without working the foot stitch. Work the outside curve stitch and return to the inner, pin up the weavers in the same pin hole as the last row and then work the edge stitch. This prevents the other threads pulling away. In cases where the curve is very sharp the turning pin hole can be used three times as shown in the diagram. Alternatively one can work with no pins on the inside, and this forms a hole as in diagram 8.

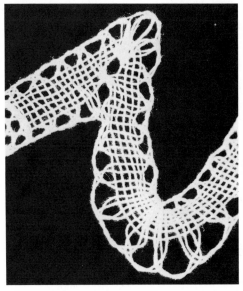

Fig. 11 ABOVE Braid with a turn for a sharp corner and a curve

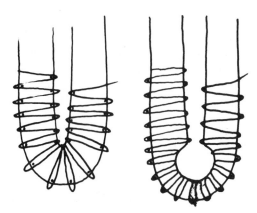

Diagram 8 Curving the braid either by using the turning pin three times or by turning with no pins on the inside edge

If the bend is very sharp, then a different technique is needed. Follow diagram 9: work to A and leave the foot pair, continue working but leave out a pair at B, C and D. Turn without pinning on the last stitch to bring the edge level with D. Work across to D and work through the pair hanging from D. Tie this pair with a single knot so that the weavers are firmly held and take the tied pair back as the new weavers. Repeat this till A is reached, pin up the weavers as before and work the edge stitch with the pair from A. Continue the braid.

Sewings

Where the braid joins itself or joins to another braid, it is necessary to do a 'sewing'. This means bringing the loop of one weaver through the pinhole of the opposite braid and passing the other bobbin of the pair through it as in diagram 10. This can be done with a fine crochet hook or a needle

Diagram 9 Turning a sharp corner

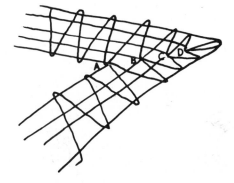

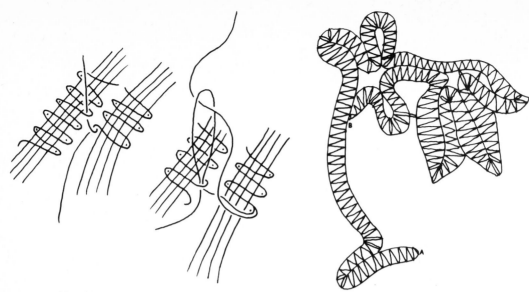

Diagram 10 Working sewings

Diagram 11 Motif which begins at A and sews out at B

Diagram 12 Collar or handkerchief corner starting at A and sewing out at B. C can have a tally inserted (see Tallies, Chapter 3)

pin, or by threading the loop through a needle and taking this up through the pinhole. Threads are sewn out by this method at the finish.

Designs 11, 12 and 13 may now be worked. Design 11 is a small motif which can be worked in Sylko 40 and can decorate a dress, 12 can be used as a corner for a handkerchief or with another for a collar and 13 is a border design which can be repeated for any length.

Decorating the Braid
The following techniques are given to make the braid more interesting and will be referred to again when shaped pieces are made in Chapter 3. Each of the movements that you make has a purpose. Twists are used to divide the

18

threads, spacing them, and the more there are the bigger the spacing. This is a useful technique for making a few threads spread out wider as in the design in diagram 12. Twists at the end of a row of cloth stitch correspond to the selvedge on a piece of material; they form loops, and the more twists the bigger the loop. These twists depend on the thread size, and one needs less twists for thick threads and more twists for thin threads. All the work is done on the wrong side of the finished article so that loose threads and knots can be planned, knowing that they will not be seen on the right side. This means that all designs have to be worked in reverse.

Dividing the Braid

This often appears in a design, for instance when dividing a tree trunk into branches. Work to the centre and one more pair, pin up the weavers, enclose the pin and work back to the edge. Take the pair hanging from the central pin and use these as the weavers on the other side.

Diagram 14 Dividing a braid

Joining Braids

Work both sides to the central pin, make a stitch with both sets of weavers and pin up into the central hole. Leave one pair hanging and use the other

Diagram 13 Continuous braid which can be used on lampshades or on dress

pair as the weavers for the joined braid.

By dividing and joining at intervals, splits can be made. Larger holes can be made by marking in the desired shape and working either side of it, joining at the bottom.

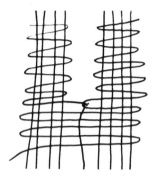

Diagram 15   Joining two braids

Half Stitch

This is a variation that forms a star-shaped weave and is a more open pattern than cloth stitch.

Set up as for the beginning braid and follow the diagrams. Begin on the right and number the threads as before. Move 2 across 3 to the right, 2 over 1 and 4 over 3 to the left. Do not complete the movement but repeat with the next pair to the left. You will notice that only one weaving thread of the pair has crossed to the other side. Pin up under a pair as before but work a whole stitch to enclose the pin; this makes a firmer edge. Cross the weavers right over left and weave across in half stitch to the other side. Continue in this way; although the pattern does not look clear at first the star shapes will gradually form. Care must be taken to keep the pairs fanned out because if they get crossed by accident a beginner will find it very difficult to sort out.

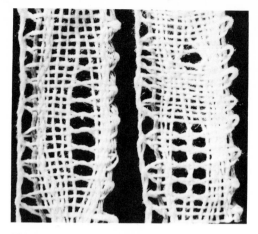

Fig. 12   ABOVE Veins in a braid

Veins

A vein can sometimes be put in the centre of a braid and there are two variants.

Vein I – for an even number of passives

Work through to the centre of the braid, twist the weavers twice and continue across. Repeat the twists below twists on every row as many times as desired. This form of vein can be shaped by twisting weavers once on the first row, twice on second and third, three times on fourth, twice on fifth and sixth and once on seventh.

Vein II – for an odd number of passives

This forms a wide vein and is suitable for wider braids. Work through to the middle pair of passives, twist these once and twist the weavers once before working through the twisted passive pair and once after. Continue to other side of braid. This centre twist can be worked on every row for as long as desired.

Holes

A single hole can be made in a braid by marking it on the pattern. Work through to the position of the hole,

20

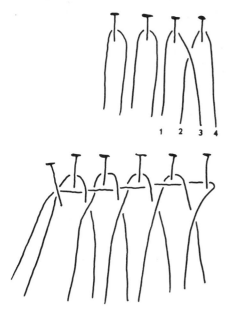
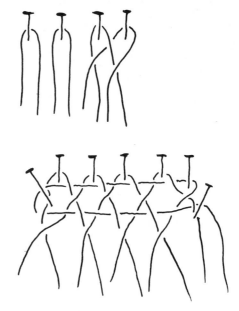

Diagram 16 Working half stitch

twist the weavers twice and place a pin under them into the marked dot; continue across the braid.

On the return journey twist the passives on either side of the pin and the weavers below the twists of the previous row. Continue the braid as before.

Windows
These form a series of holes in a line across the braid to form a division.

Work through the first pair; twist both pairs twice. Work through the second pair, twist both pairs twice; continue to do this till the last pair is reached. Work through but do not twist; pin up as usual. On the return journey twist the weavers only after each stitch.

Fig. 13 Simple hole, four pin hole and windows

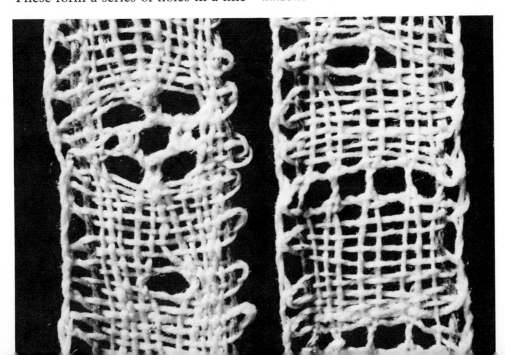

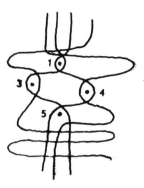

Diagram 17 Working a four pin hole

Four Pin Hole

This is marked by four dots on the pattern, usually in the centre. Work through to the centre of the braid plus one more pair. Take the last pair worked back to the edge and pin up. Take the first set of weavers out to the opposite edge and pin up. Make a whole stitch with the centre pairs and pin into hole 1; twist once. Bring both sets of weavers back to the middle, make a whole stitch with them and the two centre pairs and pin up into 2 and 3. Twist weavers once and return with them to the outside edges, pinning as before. Make a whole stitch with the two centre pairs and pin up into 4. Bring both sets of weavers to the centre again and this time select one of them as the permanent set leaving the other set as passives. The selection of the weaver depends on the position and straightness of the braid.

Gimp

A heavier thread can be used to outline and support the edge. It is kept on the edge and worked with its neighbouring thin one as a pair. Make sure that it stays in position; it should be first thread of the first pair of passives on either side of the braid. This thicker thread can be used to divide the braid by weaving one through the passives to the other side, taking it under and over the other gimp and weaving it back to its original position.

Petals or Leaves

Petals on the surface or as raised lumps on the braid can give extra dimension and can be worked in a different colour to the braid. Take the centre four threads of the braid and make a whole stitch with them. Holding them fanned out, take the second one from the left and weave it over and under the other three in turn. Hold the fanned out pairs firmly while pulling the weaving thread up after every third weave. By fanning the pairs wider or narrower, control over the width of the petal is achieved. At the required length, make a whole stitch to finish. Care must be taken to support the weaving thread as, if it is allowed to drop, the petal will lose its shape. Should this happen, support the weaver and pull the two outside threads. The shape will then be regained.

Diagram 18 Leaves or petals

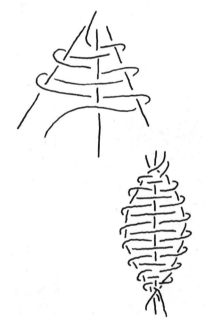

Diagram 19 A knotted picot

For a flat surface petal, pin the pairs at the end of the petal and push the pin into the pillow. Continue the braid on top of the petal with the pairs that are left until the bottom pin is reached. Work through the petal pairs when they are reached, placing them in their correct position in the braid.

For a raised lump, support the petal with a needle or match stick to keep in a roll and work through the threads as

soon as they are reached on the next braid row.

Picot Edge

Work through to the outer edge, through the foot pair, and then with a pin lift the second weaver thread, tip it to the left and pick up the first thread. Tip the pin down through the cross formed by the threads, and pull the loop up through the gap. Pin this loop in the outside hole and pull up. Continue across the braid with the foot pair, exchanging it for the picot pair on the next row.

Picot edge of a different colour

The pattern for the braid should have two rows of dots on the outer edge. The braid goes on as usual with no foot pair on the outer edge. The edge is worked separately with one pair of passives and a weaver of a different

Diagram 20 Making a picot in a different colour

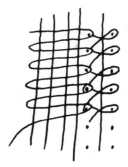

Fig. 14 Surface petal and raised petal

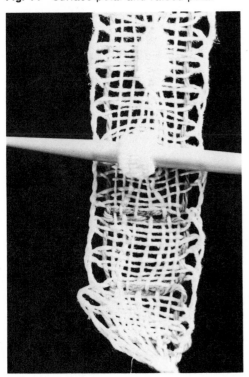

colour. This weaver goes out through the passive pair, does a picot and returns to the inner pin hole where it meets the weaver from the braid. Make a whole stitch and pin up into the hole. Enclose the pin with a whole stitch. The braid weaver continues the braid and the edge weaver does the picot; they meet each time at the inner pin hole. In this way the coloured edge can be kept separate.

Crossing Braids

Sometimes braids need to be crossed and here a sewing is necessary. As soon as the braids meet, take a sewing with the weavers into the under braid. Weave to the other side and take another sewing. Weave across and sew into the other side of the braid and again at the other edge as in the diagram (four sewings in all).

Diagram 21   Crossing braids

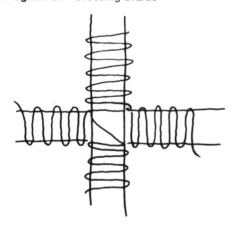

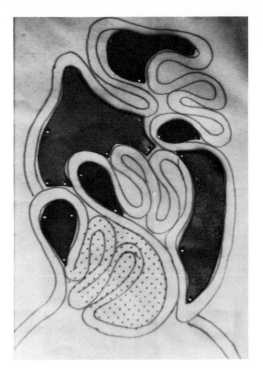

Fig. 15   ABOVE Pricking for necklace with the suede pinned into position prior to working. A filling is dotted in over the braid but the braid is worked first and the filling over it

Suede or Leather Insertions

Attractive pieces can be made by using suede or felt to fill in the open areas; the braid is worked round them. The necklace and the butterfly are worked this way. First pin the suede shapes right sides down to the pattern. Work the braid till the shapes are reached, thread the loop of the top weaver

through a needle and pull it through the suede. Thread the other weaver through the loop and pull up; a sewing like this must be made on every row as the braid rounds the suede. These suede areas can be decorated with embroidery afterwards.

Any design which is continuous can be worked in this way and inspiration can come from ancient works of art, pottery and paintings, primitive drawings and some crewel embroidery.

Once the principle of working is understood it should not be difficult to design continuous patterns.

Diagram 22 The butterfly can be worked in Sylko. Start with 10 pairs at A. Divide the braid at B and work both sides, making long sewings as shown and joining at C. D shows the position of the suede. This area could have filling stitches inserted

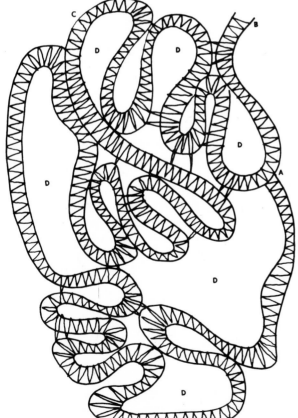

Diagram 23 Necklace started at A. B continues for the neck width, sews out at C. Areas D are for suede or filling stitches

THREE

Fillings

Meshes Plaited grounds Meshes with cloth stitch Spider grounds Grounds with tallies

In order to make designs more interesting and to fill the spaces created by the design, the technique of working fillings is introduced. These make use of the stitches already learnt but in a different sequence.

The bobbins are linked into the body of the work with sewings, and their position is usually directly above the marked holes of the filling. The pricking or marking for each filling is worked out on graph paper for accuracy before transferring it to the design. The size of graph paper and thus the width apart of the pinholes depends on the size of the space, the size of thread and the denseness of the required filling. Fillings give more texture and life to a design, forming shade and light, therefore their choice needs care. They are in five groups: meshes, meshes with some cloth stitch areas, plaited meshes, spider grounds and petal or tally formations.

Each filling is shown being worked within a square, and a beginner will find it useful to make a sample of each, joining them together in patchwork form to make an attractive sampler panel.

Most shapes within a design are irregular, and marking the filling needs special care. Draw the design onto tracing paper and place the open areas over the graphed-out filling so that the best position is found. It is better to work from the centre, planning this first. Some fillings are worked horizontally and some diagonally, so that the lead thread weaver from one side will be sewn in on the other, often left hanging as a passive or tied off. In a horizontal filling the lead thread will work across, be sewn out and return as lead thread on the next row. This will all become apparent as you work.

The pricking given for the squares can be worked in 1 ply wool, Sylko Perle 12, Coton à Broder 18, Fil à Dentelle, D.M.C. 20 or any thread of similar weight. If a thinner thread is used prickings must be plotted smaller, otherwise the result will be very open.

Make the square shape first with five pairs, a foot on the outside only and in a twisted cloth stitch. This makes a firm outer shape which will not stretch when joining at the end.

Begin at the left hand corner, using the corner pin hole three times as you turn each corner and changing to plain cloth stitch with no twists on the three rows as you turn. Tie off the threads in the left hand corner when you reach it; one or two pairs can start the filling and the others can be cut off.

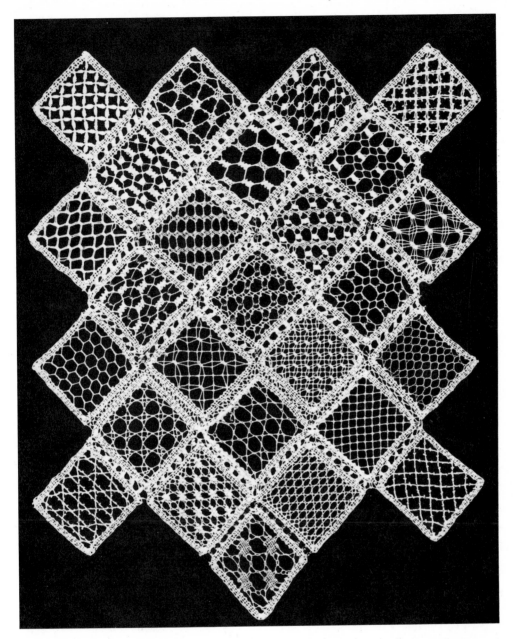

Fig. 16 A SAMPLER OF STITCHES. FROM LEFT TO RIGHT IN ROWS FROM THE TOP:
(i) Maltese leaves, Bedfordshire spider, Honeycomb with tallies, Plaited leaves
(ii) Toad in the hole, Snatch bar, Lattice and cutwork
(iii) Open spider, Striped ground, Striped ground with tallies, Flemish spider
(iv) Toad in the hole with beads, Striped ground with beads, Lattice and cutwork with beads
(v) Brussels, Torchon spider, Torchon spider pricked finer, Lille
(vi) Rose ground, Honeycomb, Torchon
(vii) Plaits eternal, Mayflower worked fine, Honeycomb worked fine, Simple plait
(viii) Mayflower

Sewings

Pairs are sewn in to the braid by pulling the loop of the pair through the pin hole of the braid and passing one bobbin of the pair through it. Two pairs can be sewn in by placing another pair across the loop and taking both bobbins through the loop as in diagram 24.

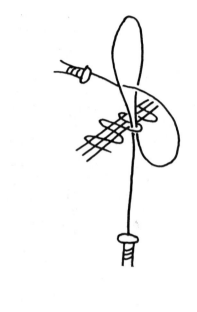

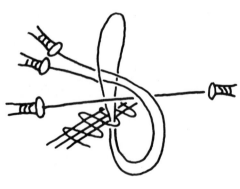

Diagram 24 Sewing one or two pairs into the braid for a filling

MESHES

Torchon

Hang in two pairs at b, c, d, e and f and one pair at a and g. Make a half stitch with the pair from a and the pair from b; pin in the hole diagonally from a. Make another half stitch to enclose the pin and take the left hand pair to sew out at h. Return to the top edge and take the pair from c, work the diagonal, half stitch, pin up, half stitch in each hole, sewing out at i. Continue to work the diagonals, following the diagram, d to j, e to k, f to i, and g to m. The next diagonal row will be worked with the pair from f, sewn in at n and worked to o.

Continue working the diagonals, sewing in to the sides and tying out at the base in their correct place.

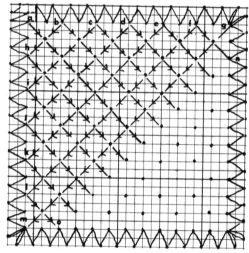

Diagram 25 Torchon or Lille

Lille or Point Ground

This is worked from the same pricking as torchon but is traditionally pricked at 55° or 60° instead of 45°. The difference is in the shape of the net hole formed.

The square is worked diagonally as with torchon but the stitch is different. It consists of a half stitch with three twists, pinned up but not enclosed, making a very stretchy net.

Honeycomb

This is a filling found in many point ground patterns and is usually pricked at 55° or 60°. The sample is worked at 45° and the stitch is half stitch and twist, pin up, half stitch and twist diagonally.

Hang on one pair at a, c, d, f, g and i and two pairs at b, e and h. Start at b and make a half stitch and twist with the pair from a. Pin up and make another half stitch and twist to enclose the pin. Sew out at j and leave it as a passive for the next row. The next diagonal row is a short one. A pair from b works with a pair from c and k and the pair from the previous row works with the pair from j to form l. The third diagonal is a long row beginning with e and d and sewing out at m.

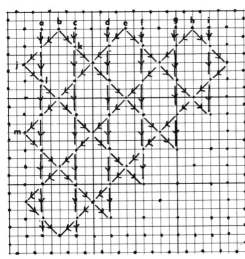

Diagram 26 Honeycomb

Work each pair as you come to them. Continue the short row and the long row sewing in to the sides and tying out at the base. The sample is shown pricked and worked at $\frac{2}{10}$ but can be made much denser if pricked at $\frac{1}{10}$.

Rose Ground

This filling is worked in squares. Each block is then worked on the diagonal (see diagram 27).

Take the two pairs from a and make a half stitch but do not pin up; do the same with the two pairs from b. Make a half stitch with the centre pairs of the four and pin into hole 1. Take the two pairs to the left and work a half stitch, pin up, half stitch into hole 2 and the two pairs to the right, half stitch, pin up, half stitch into hole 3.

Finally, take the centre pairs again and make a half stitch, pin up, half stitch into hole 4. Work each block diagonally and do not forget to make the half stitch without pinning before you start the square 1, 2, 3, 4.

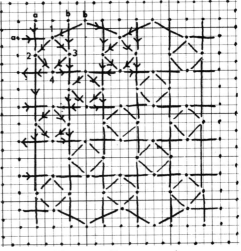

Diagram 27 ABOVE Rose ground
Diagram 28 BELOW Working rose ground

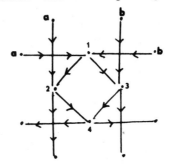

29

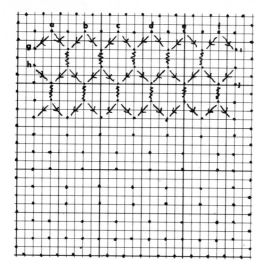

Diagram 29 Brussels or Mechlin

Diagram 30 Making a plait

Diagram 31 Working a windmill crossing

Brussels or Mechlin

This mesh is worked horizontally. Hang two pairs at a, b, c, d, e and f. Twist the pair from a once and sew into the side at g and again at h to bring it in line for the next row. Do the same with the pair from f at i and j. Twist the pairs from a and b once and make a whole stitch. Pin up into hole k and enclose with a whole stitch. Make another whole stitch and pin this up in hole l, enclose with a whole stitch.

This forms a short plait from k to l. Do the same with the pairs c and d and e and f. Work horizontal rows as in the diagram, sewing in at the sides and tying out at the base.

PLAITED GROUNDS

Instead of twists, these grounds have half stitch plaits and 'windmill' joins where they meet. The plaits usually have picots on them.

Plaits

With two pairs of bobbins, work a half stitch, then another one. Take a pair of bobbins in each hand and pull the stitches tight. Repeat this until the plait thus formed is the right length.

Windmill join

This occurs when eight threads (four pairs) meet, join and divide. Take the four pairs and treat each pair as one thread. Make a half stitch, put up a pin and then complete the move by crossing 2 over 3 to enclose the pin. Continue the plaits.

Picots

The knotted picots can be used but it is often simpler to pin a loop at the required side, either right or left.

Right side: put a pin in the marked hole and take the outside thread of the plait round it anti-clockwise; continue plaiting.

Left side: put a pin in the marked hole and take the outside thread on the left round it clockwise; continue plaiting.

Simple Plait

Hang two pairs on a and d and four pairs on b and c. Following the diagram, plait from a to the two dots and make a picot on either side; continue plaiting to e. Make another plait from b and do a windmill join at e, plait to f and sew both pairs to the side and leave. Work the whole filling following the directional arrows.

Plaits Eternal

This plaited filling is found frequently in France and is worked both horizontally and diagonally. Each plaited bar has a picot on it either to left or right as marked and the windmill joins are made wherever plaits meet. Plaits are worked horizontally from d to e, sewn out at e and again at f and return on the next horizontal row f to g. Follow the diagram for direction.

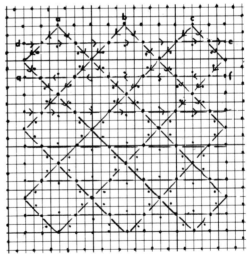

Diagram 33 Plaits eternal

Plaited Leaves

This can be worked either horizontally or diagonally. The leaf is formed by two plaits with picots on their outsides meeting another two plaits at a centre, forming a flower.

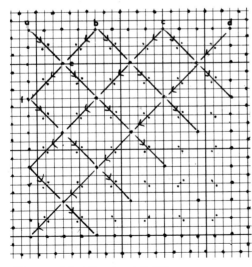

Diagram 32 Simple plait filling

31

Hang in four pairs at a and e and eight pairs at b, c and d. Work small plaits down to the picot holes; make a left picot on one and a right picot on the other. Join all the plaits at f, g and h with a four plait crossing and sew out at the sides for the next row. The joins need to be pulled tight as this forms a dense pattern.

Four plait crossing
Treat each pair as one bobbin as in the windmill, although the sequence is more complicated.

Work a half stitch with the centre four pairs, work a half stitch with the right hand four pairs and then with the left hand four pairs. Work another half stitch with the centre four pairs and pin up to support. Half stitch the right hand four pairs and then the left hand four pairs. Make a whole stitch with the centre four pairs and then cross the second of the eight pairs over the third and the sixth over the seventh.

MESHES WITH CLOTH STITCH

Mayflower
This is worked on a honeycomb pricking and can be at 60° instead of 45° as it is a Bucks filling. Solid cloth stitch diamonds are worked at alternate intervals to make a spotted mesh. Hang in as for honeycomb and work a and b to j. Work k and l, g and h to form m, and h and i to make n. The pairs are now ready to work the diamond d, e, f. Work the diamond in cloth stitch following the directional arrows. With the pair from e, work through the pair from d and pin up at o, turn with a twist and work back through the pair from e and pick up the pair from f pinning up at p. Turn with a twist and work back through the pairs to pick up the pair from k at

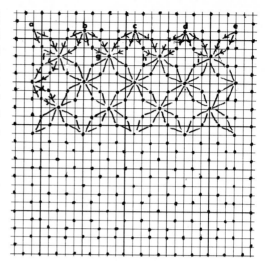

Diagram 34 Plaited leaves

q, turn and work back to r picking up a pair from m. Work s, t and u in the same way but leave out pairs at q, r, s and t to continue the mesh. There should be two pairs left at the bottom of the diamond. The pair from s and u works the honeycomb stitch to form v so that the next diamond can be worked. Continue the filling following the arrows.

Striped Ground
Hang in one pair at a, b, d, e, g, and h and two pairs at c, f and i. Begin at c and with one pair make a whole stitch with the pair from d at k. Weave to the right, through the other pair from c, and pick up the pair from a at l, leaving a pair out at k for the next diagonal row. Weave across to m and back to n, leaving another pair out at m and picking up the pair from b. Sew out at the edge where indicated at o and p. Continue in this way, taking pairs in on the right and leaving them out on the left. Work diagonal rows g, f, q and i, j, r and sew in at the base and side as is necessary. This filling can be worked in cloth stitch or half stitch as desired.

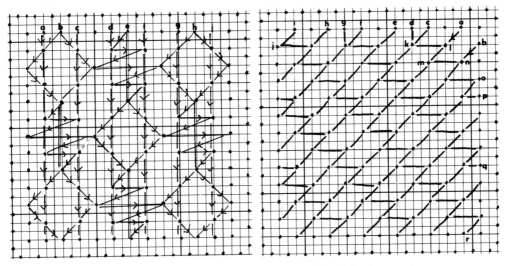

Diagram 35 Mayflower

Diagram 36 Striped ground

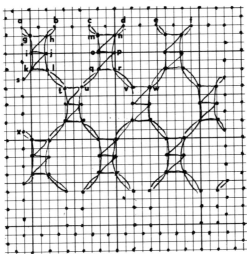

Diagram 37 Snatch bar

Snatch Bar

This is a Honiton filling and consists of small cloth stitch blocks joined by small plaits. The twists at the end of each cloth stitch row form a loop which gives a picot edge to the block.

Hang in two pairs at a, b, c, d, e and f and make short plaits with each two pairs to the first pin holes. Put a pin between the plait from a into g, enclose it with a whole stitch and work across to the right through the plait from b. Twist five times and pin up at h, turn and work back to i, twist five and return to j, back to k and then to l. Divide the threads and plait to s and t. Work the cloth block mn to qr and plait to v and u. Work the next bar tu and continue diagonally, sewing in to the side as is necessary.

Bedfordshire Spider

These are small solid areas in either whole or half stitch, joined by plaits with picots. Each solid block can have a raised tally in its centre for further decoration.

Hang in two pairs at a, b, c, d, e, f and g. Begin in the left corner and, using the pair from a as weavers, work half stitch through the pairs from b and c, pin up in h, turn and work back to i, pin up and return to j, leaving two pairs out at h and two pairs out at i for the next block. Plait from i to k and sew out at k and again at l. Work e, f, g in the same way, plaiting to m and sewing in. Work the plait from d to p putting in the picots, and work the second row block with this and the plaits from k and n. Work the rows horizontally.

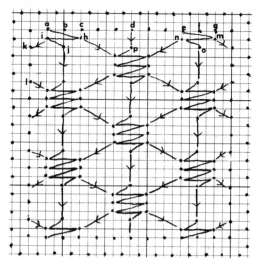

Diagram 38 Bedfordshire spiders

SPIDER GROUNDS

A spider is formed by using the threads from one side of a diamond shaped space and crossing them through the threads on the other side in whole stitch. They are pinned into position in the centre hole and worked back to their original position. This forms a body in the centre and legs coming from it. The more threads that there are the fatter will be the body. Each pair is twisted three times and each pair in turn passes through the others, as in the diagram.

Open

Hang on two pairs at a and e and four pairs at b, c, and d. Twist each pair three times and make a spider with pairs a and b pinning into f, b and c into g, c and d into h and d and e into i. This can be worked horizontally or diagonally following the directional arrows. Sew into the sides where necessary and tie out at the base.

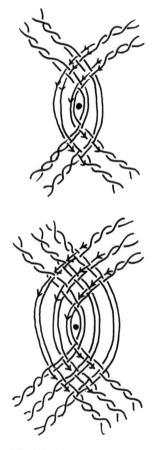

Diagram 39 Working spiders

34

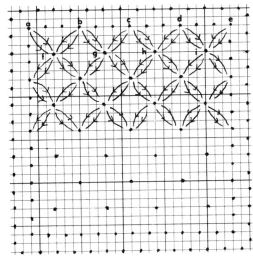

Diagram 40 Open spider ground

Torchon Spider

Hang in two pairs at a, b, d and e and four pairs at c. Twist the two pairs from a three times and leave. With the pair from b make a half stitch, pin up, half stitch, with the leg from a into f. Repeat this with the pair from f and the other leg from a pinned into g and sewn out at h. In the same way work from b to i, j and k, d to l, m and k and d to n, o, and p. Twist the spider legs from f, g, i and j, three times and make the spider at q. Similarly make the spider at r. Pick up the legs of the spider at q into s and t with a half stitch, pin up, half stitch, with the pair from h and into k, u and v with the pair from k. The pair from v and t meet at w. This encloses the spider.

Continue working the spiders following the arrows. This ground can be made more dense by making the pricking at $\frac{1}{10}$ instead of $\frac{2}{10}$.

Flemish Spider

The spiders in this ground have three pairs of legs on each side joining to make a bigger body and twelve legs at the end. It is worked similarly to the open spider, but where the legs meet from the other spider they cross with a whole stitch and twist without pinning. Hang on one pair at a, b, c, j, k, and l and two pairs at d, e and f and g, h and i. Following the diagram, work spiders at m, n and o working whole stitch and a twist through the pairs where they meet at d, e, f and at g, h, i, and at p and q. Remember to twist three times before and after the spider's body is worked.

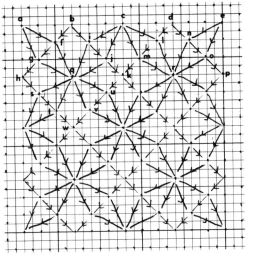

Diagram 41 Torchon spider

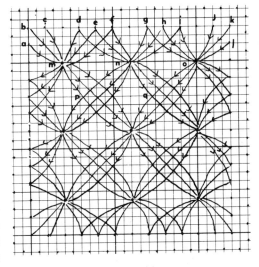

Diagram 42 Flemish spider

Diagram 43
Working a tally

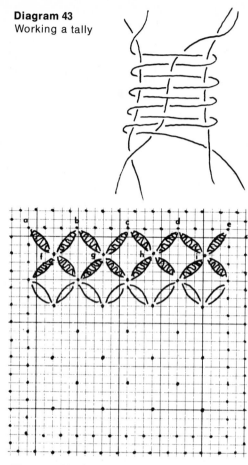

Diagram 44 Maltese leaves

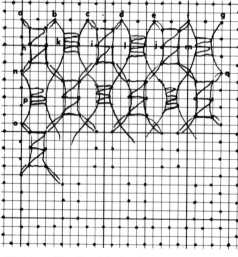

Diagram 45 Toad in the hole

GROUNDS WITH TALLIES

Tallies or leaves can be put wherever there are two pairs of threads hanging separated by a stitch. Leaves are always worked with a whole stitch at the beginning and end of the weave, but tallies are worked without either and are kept very square (see diagram 43).

Maltese Leaves

Hang two pairs on a and e and four pairs on b, c and d. Weave a leaf with the pairs from a and a leaf with the pairs from b. Make a windmill join where they meet at f; pull up tightly as this is quite a dense ground. Make leaves from b and c, c and d, and d and e, joining at g, h and i. Continue the filling horizontally or diagonally taking great care to make the leaves of even size by having the same number of weaves on each.

Toad in the Hole

This is another traditional Honiton filling worked as a variation to the snatch bar. The tallies are worked in between the bars and their threads cross diagonally.

Hang on two pairs at a and three pairs at b, c, d, e and f, and one pair at g. Work a snatch bar at h, i and j as in the snatch bar filling. Make tallies with a pair from b and c, d and e, and f and g. Support with a pin under them if you are a beginner. Twist the pairs three times and work them through the plait of the snatch bar with a whole stitch to make the tally on the row below. This can be worked horizontally or diagonally and the two pairs sewn out at h come in for the tally at p. The other pair is sewn in again at o for the next snatch. Another pair needs to be added at q for the snatch of the second row.

Cutwork and Lattice

This is another Honiton filling; cutwork is the traditional name for a tally.

Hang in a pair at a and g and two pairs at b, c, d, e and f. Work a whole stitch, pin up, whole stitch into h with a and b, into i with b and c, into k with d and e, into l with e and f and into m with f and g.

Make a tally with the inner pair from h and i, then make a whole stitch with a tally pair and the other pair from h and i pinning into n and o.

Similarly work the tally j and k and l and m; pins at t, u, v, w and x are made to form the lattice from the pairs above, sewing into the side as is necessary. Work the filling horizontally alternating the tallies and following the directional arrows on the diagram.

Striped Ground with Tallies

The stripes formed by this ground can have tallies put between the rows diagonally (see diagram).

Fig. 17 ABOVE Reverse side of the seaweed panel showing tape worked through the suede and the filling over the braid underneath

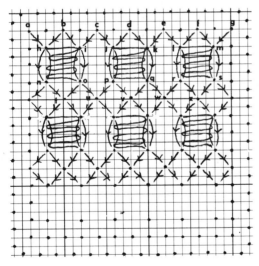

Diagram 46 ABOVE Cutwork and lattice

Diagram 47 RIGHT Striped ground with tallies

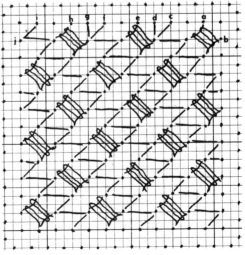

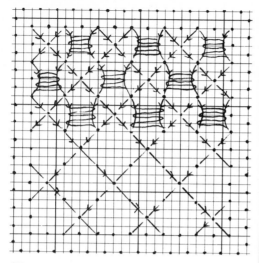

Diagram 48   Honeycomb with tallies

Honeycomb with Tallies

The tallies are placed alternately on the short row as in the diagram. Anywhere that a tally is used, it can be replaced by a bead. Work a sewing through the hole in the bead by putting the loop of one bobbin through

Fig. 18   Panel used on a bag; fawn, brown and gold

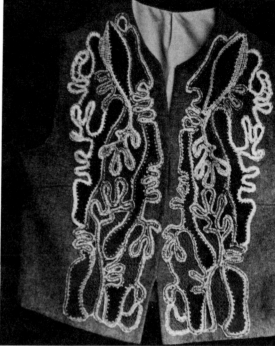

Fig. 19   Seaweed panel used on a waistcoat in natural and brown with red and brown suede

the hole with a needle and threading the other bobbin through it.

The pattern for the seaweed panel is worked with suede inserts and filling stitches of torchon and rose ground to form a continuous decoration. The pattern is reversed to form the whole length or it can be repeated several times. It is illustrated on a waistcoat and on a bag, and will make a set with the necklace.

Diagram 49   Sewing in a bead with two pairs of bobbins

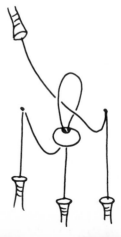

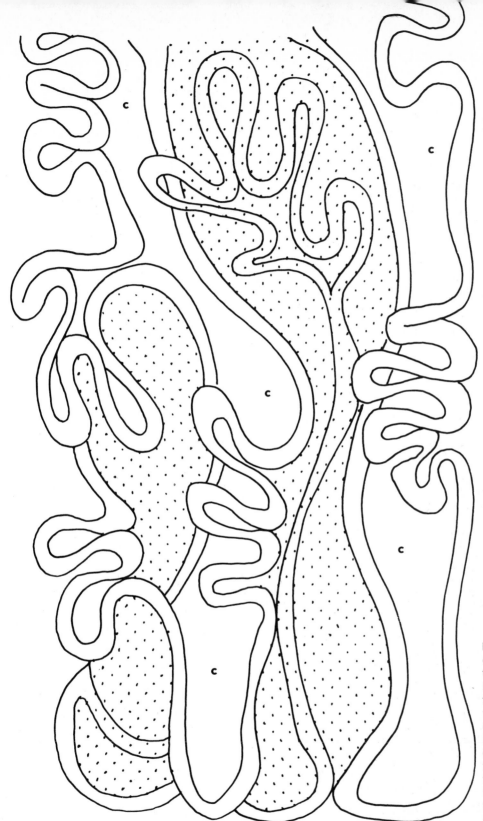

Diagram 50 Seaweed design marked out for torchon ground. Each braid is continuous; follow it through to see where to begin and end. The pattern can be reversed to form a continuous panel. All the braid is worked first through the suede insets and the filling worked last over parts of the braid

39

Fig. 20 Silk flower in cream and gold with a variety of fillings

Fig. 21 Flower opened out to form a petal collar. Gathering thread round the top is pulled up to produce the flower. Worked as a combination of tape form and one piece lace

FOUR

Adapted Honiton Techniques

Leaves   Flowers   Butterflies and moths Birds   Trees   Figures and animals

The cloth stitch braids are now shaped so that more complicated designs can be worked. These will take the shape of any piece that is drawn provided that there are enough threads in it to make it firm. Threads can be added and subtracted where necessary, but usually on the outside curve. There is a limit to the cloth stitch area that can be worked both comfortably and neatly and it is often necessary to break wide areas up with sewings or fillings. It is possible to work any shape in lace and instructions are given for working leaves, flowers, stalks, trees, butterflies, birds, fish, animals, people and buildings. The size given can be enlarged or diminished depending on the thread selected or the purpose of the finished piece. The size illustrated is suitable for Sylko, Fil à Dentelle, one ply wool, one strand of Anchor stranded cotton or DMC Brilliante 20 or 30.

LEAVES

There are many different leaf shapes: long and thin, round, indented, palmate and multiple. All can be worked in lace stitches in white or colour shading.

Simple Leaf

This shape has been drawn for technique purposes, but each leaf on a plant varies.

Begin by setting up three pairs on pin a, work through in whole stitch to the left and pin up at b. Add a pair by hanging them on pin b to the right of the weavers and working through them; these will be the foot pair. Pairs can be added in this way when there is to be no foot. Work back to c and add another pair for the foot on the right. Work back and forth once more, pinning up the weavers before the last pair is worked and then working through these for the foot. Begin adding pairs on every row till there are twelve pairs at d.

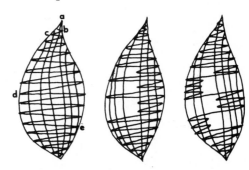

Diagram 51   Simple leaves in various cloth stitch weaves

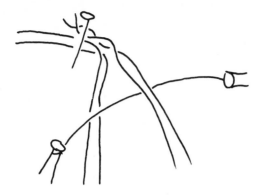

Diagram 52 Adding a pair

Adding pairs

Follow diagram 52, and before working the foot stitch bring the new pair under the foot pair up to the pin and place them in position to the left of the pin and the weavers. Work the foot stitch and the new pair will be held in place. Pairs can be added in the centre by placing a pin in the required position and hanging a pair on it; work through it when weaving across but do not take the pin out. This is useful when adding coloured threads when a change in shade is needed or to add extra pairs when working a raised petal or tally.

Work the leaf without adding up to e; now decrease pairs by putting the third pair or second to last pair out and back over the leaf to be cut off later. Continue till there are five pairs left to work a stalk. This leaf can have vari-

Fig. 22 Leaves worked in various forms

Fig. 23 Leaves with holes and open middles from a panel designed by Elena Holeczyova

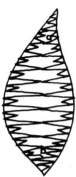   

Diagram 53 Leaf with a centre made by meeting the weavers; **54** Leaf with an open centre for a filling; **55** Leaf with an open centre with maltese leaves worked simultaneously; **56** Leaf with a plaited and picot edge

ants in weave as shown, it can have veins, holes or picots, or be worked in half stitch.

It can be further decorated by using a thicker gimp thread at the edges or as a raised vein in the centre.

Leaves with Open Centres
These leaves are more lace-like and can be worked in two different ways.

1. Begin as for the simple leaf until eight pairs are on. Work to the centre, through three pairs and put in a pin at a; enclose with a whole stitch. One of these pairs is the weaver for the left and the other is the weaver for the right. Work both sides simultaneously, meeting and working the weavers together in a whole stitch on alternate rows as shown in the diagram. This has a foot on the outside but no foot on the inside. Meet the pairs again at b and decrease to five for the stalk. This leaf looks attractive with the weavers making a tally when they meet or by putting in a bead where they meet.

2. This open leaf has two sides worked separately, keeping a foot on the inside and the outside of the leaf, needing 10 pairs. The leaf divides at a and joins again at b for the stalk. When the leaf shape is finished pairs can be added again to make any of the fillings of the previous chapter. These could be in a different tone or colour to the main part.

Leaf with Maltese Leaf Centre
Work as for the open leaves and divide at a; add one pair at b and c on the inside of the leaf by placing a pair on the pin inside the weavers and working through them. The two new pairs twist twice and make a plait to d. Add two pairs at e, make a maltese leaf and do a windmill join at d with the plaited stalk. Make a Maltese leaf from d to f. When the weavers on the right side reach f work them through the leaf from d carrying them in the workings until g. Leave them out at g and work Maltese leaves and a windmill from g to h. The leaf at h is taken in on the left hand side and then left out at i. Continue to the bottom of the leaf decreasing to five and joining the plaited stalk in at j.

Leaf with a Fancy Edge
This leaf is made in the same way as the simple leaf but has a plait with picots going in and out of the cloth as shown. It can be done simultaneously or it can be added afterwards by sewings.

43

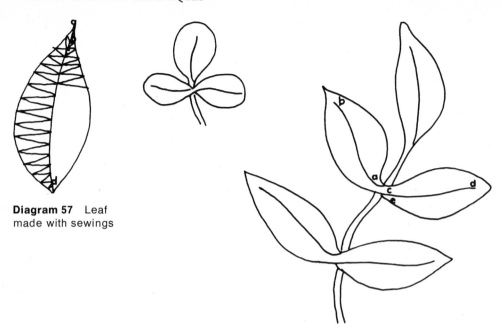

Diagram 57 Leaf
made with sewings

Diagram 58 Making sprays with sewings

Diagram 59 Leaves
with multiple sewings

Leaves with Sewings

A very interesting leaf can be made by working up one side of it and back down the other, making sewings on the centre vein. One can have whole stitch on one side and half stitch on the other, thus giving light and shade. This leaf requires half the number of bobbins but it takes longer to do because of the sewings. It enables one to make a spray of leaves without tying off each time.

A single leaf is started at the stalk end with five pairs, increasing to seven or eight on the outside curve. The number depends on the size of thread. Work to the top of the leaf, turning as for a sharp corner, and leaving a pair out at a, b, and c and using the last pin hole three times to turn level with c. Begin half stitch at c and begin sewings after pin a is reached. Decrease to the minimum number of pairs (three) and sew out at d.

44

To make a spray, work the stalk in a five-pair braid until the top leaf is reached; work this leaf and tie off the threads. Sew in five pairs at a, work the leaf, turning at b, with seven pairs. Do not decrease unless really necessary but rather squash them through c for the opposite leaf and work up to d. Turn and decrease pairs down to the minimum to tie out at e. Repeat for the next pair of leaves. A clover leaf can be done in this way as in diagram 58.

Leaves with Multiple Sewings

These are the palmate group and are worked as a continuous braid, increasing and decreasing the width as necessary. Both leaves begin at a and tie out at b, working sharp or curved turns as the shape demands.

Indented Leaves

These can be worked in two different ways and will look different.

1. Set up three pairs and increase on both sides to give nine pairs at a. Divide to give four to the left and five to the right. Work both sides simultaneously so that sewings can be made at intervals across the opening in the centre. Increase to six pairs on either side and leave two pairs out at b and e and one pair out at c, d, f and g. Leave the weavers at h and i pinned to wait until the two serrations j and k are worked. Begin these at the tips j and k with the two pairs that have been left out at b and e, picking up pairs c and d and f and g as they are reached. When you are level with h and i take the weavers from the serrations straight across through the pinned up weavers at h and i to the centre. Continue in this way to the base decreasing to three pairs on either side where they meet at l.

2. Set up as for 1 but increase to ten

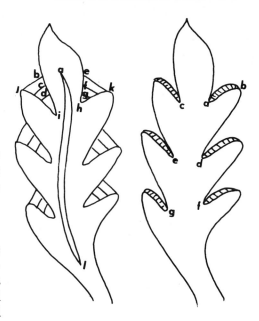

Diagram 60   Indented leaves

pairs. At a leave out three pairs and leave the weavers hanging at a. Twist the three pairs to form a loose rope up to b, pin them up at b, and work the serration down to a, making a sewing through the roped threads when they are reached. At a take the weavers from the serration through the pinned weavers on to c. Leave out three pairs at c and work the left serration in the same way as for the right. Continue down to d, then e, f and g, repeating the serrations and adding another two pairs as the leaf widens. The leaf looks more interesting if a twisted vein is made in the centre, starting it just below the first set of serrations. Decrease to five pairs for the stalk.

Leaves in Colour

These can be made by all the various methods but there are a few points to watch.

1. Leaves can be shaded light, medium and dark but the weavers need to be either light or a neutral

45

shade and thinner than the rest to avoid a tartan appearance.

2. Multi-coloured half stitch does not look effective as the weaver wanders too much.

3. Leaves with sewings look better with dark pairs on the inside forming a dark area to the centre which gives the illusion of dimension.

4. Diagram 61 shows a leaf with a dark pair introduced in the centre by placing a pair on a pin at a and other pairs at b and c.

through two pairs, twist the unworked pair twice and make the edge stitch (foot). Work back through one pair, then work a whole stitch and a half, 2 over 3, 4 over 3, 2 over 1, 2 over 3 then 4 over 3, 2 over 1, 2 over 3, through the last pair. Pull the threads tight and return to the pin hole with the second pair. This turning stitch does change one of the weavers so that care needs to be taken when using colour. Sewings must be made where the tendril crosses itself.

Diagram 61 Leaf with coloured threads

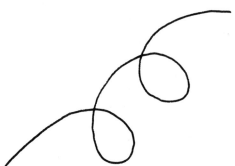

Diagram 62 A tendril

Stalks

These are no more than a simple braid with or without a foot and of the desired width.

Tendrils or Curved Stems

These are narrow and need a special technique to make them keep their curved shape. They are worked with only one set of pin holes and were known as 10-stick in Honiton as only 10 bobbins were needed. If one uses a thicker thread, three pairs are the minimum. The pins are set on the outside curve and a tendril is best started at its tip to avoid having to tie off at this weak point.

Set up four pairs on a pin and work

FLOWERS

These can be made by using various leaf shapes and combining them with stalks or tendrils. Many interesting flowers can be worked in this way.

Diagram 63(a) shows a double sewn leaf starting at a and tying out at b; a small braid is sewn in at c and out at d.

Diagram 63(b) shows a series of small stems and both could be enhanced with fillings in the spaces.

Diagram 63(c) shows a flower with petals bent back, consisting of continuous leaf shapes started at a and sewn out at b; the stamens are tendrils that turn on themselves at the tips.

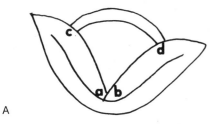

A

B

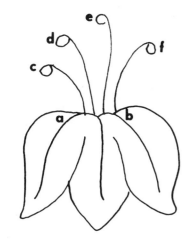

C

Diagram 63 Flowers composed of leaf shapes

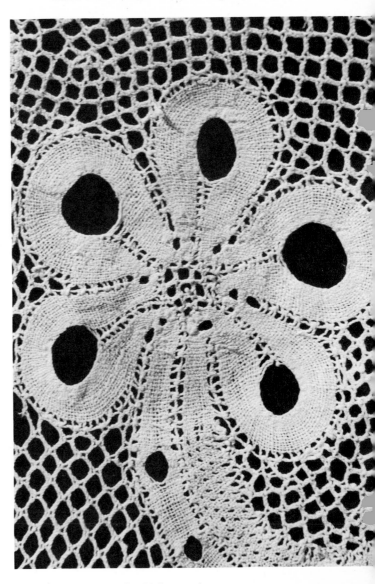

Fig. 24 Continuous braid flower shape on a Milanese flounce

Begin these at c, d, e and f, tying out on the flower.

Several leaf shapes can be made and put together on a wire stem to make a dimensional flower as in fig. 24. Smaller, rounder leaves form the buds and any variety of flower can be interpreted by observing the shapes of natural flowers.

47

Diagram 64 Continuous braid flowers

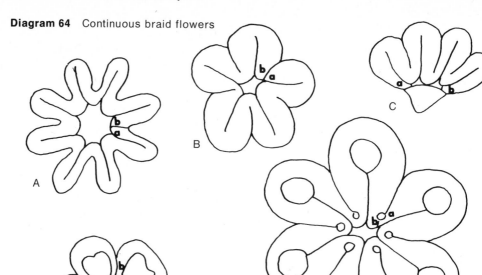

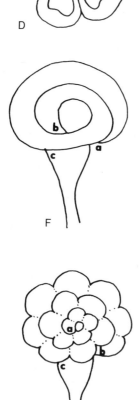

Continuous Braid Flowers

These cover numerous shapes and, by changing the width and position, varying angles of flower can be depicted.

Diagram 64(a). This is a continuous narrow braid turning tightly with sewings to give a small centre.

Diagram 64(b). This is worked in the same way as diagram 64(a) but is a wider braid and has five petals; start both at a and sew out at b.

Diagram 64(c). This is an upturned flower worked as for diagram 63(c) but it has a calyx at the base. If turned upside down the calyx can be the raised centre, as in a daisy.

Diagram 64(d). This has a centre of narrow braid which turns sharply to form the outer petals; these can have fillings added.

Diagram 64(e). This is worked as for diagram 64(b), but the turning circle on the outer and inner is worked with no pin on the inside edge as when working tendrils. This produces a

48

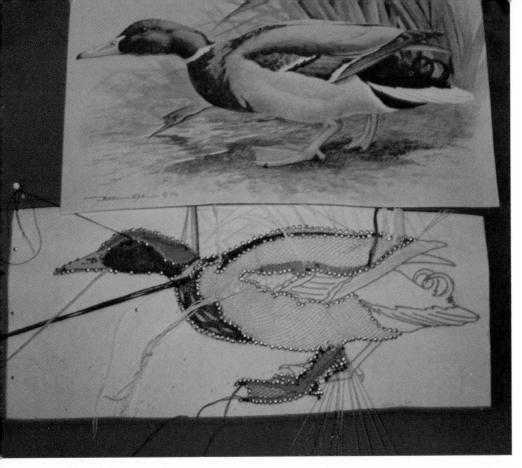

LEFT Mallard duck under construction from a coloured drawing, worked by Jan Stiny

BELOW Panel of autumn trees used as a screen

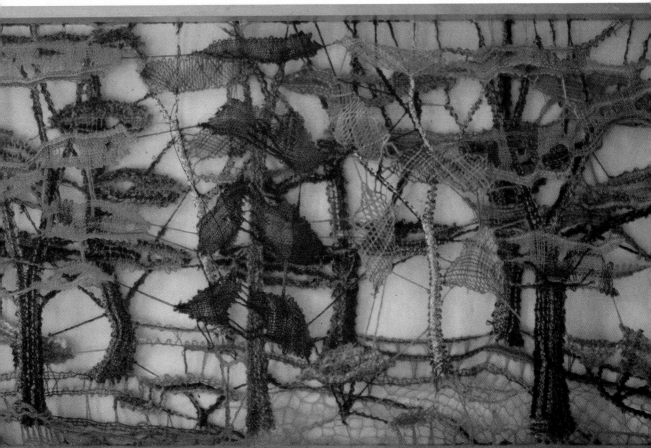

LEFT A selection of dimensional insects worked as decorative jewellery in gold and coloured threads

RIGHT Madonna and child designed from a stained glass window and worked by Margaret Kitson

LEFT Decorative uses of coloured lace as dress decoration and accessories

OPPOSITE Heron, worked in Sylko and mounted to give a three-dimensional effect

Birds of Paradise

Fig. 25 RIGHT A spray of three-dimensional flowers designed and worked by Joyce Wilmott made up of various leaf-shaped forms with stamens attached to covered wire stalks

large hole as in fig. 24.

Diagram 64(f). This is a flower of the convolvulus type. Begin at a with three pairs and widen gradually to six pairs. Make sewings at every point of contact and finally sew out at b; the threads can then be used to make a filling. The calyx and stalk are made by adding threads from a to c.

Diagram 64(g). The carnation or chrysanthemum is made in the same way as diagram 64(e) but the braid is indented by shaping it this way and by putting a gimp thread on either side and crossing where the petals indent.

Rose Shapes

Roses and water lily types are made with an indented braid and gimp and look attractive if worked alternately whole and half stitch.

Diagram 65(a). Begin at a and gradually increase as necessary when the petal widens. Pin holes will need to be closer on the inside to allow for the curve, and the petal size will need reducing as the centre is approached. The petals turn at b as neat as possible to finally sew out at c. These pairs can be used for the filling.

Diagram 65(b). A rose at a different angle is worked as a continuous indented braid but with a slight difference. It is started at a, pairs increased as necessary and decreased at b. Some pairs are sewn out and some are taken into the inner braid at c. These are finally sewn out at d.

Diagram 65(c). This is a water lily and starts at point a; pairs are added on both sides until the braid is level at bc. It turns at d and reduces, sewing out at e.

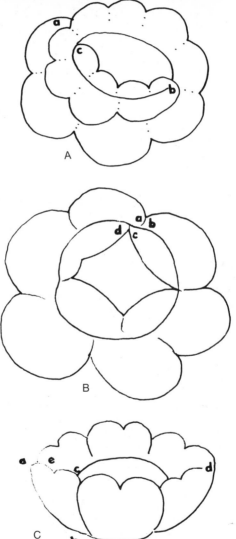

Diagram 65 Rose shapes

49

Diagram 66   Large daisy

Large Daisy

This shows how a change in the angle will give perspective to a flower. It starts at a and is sewn out at b, calyx and centre filling are worked afterwards and threads can be carried over the lower petal.

Flower Spray

This has a Jacobean appearance and can be worked larger on a cushion or in its present size as a picture or as dress decoration. Begin with the leaf forms on the large flower; they start at a and sew out at b. Make the indented petals on this flower. The threads of

Diagram 67   Flower spray

50

the one from c sew out at d but can be carried over the leaf and sewn in again at e. They sew in at f, on to g and finally sew out at h.

Make the bud in a similar way but the threads at b can continue the stalk. The other flower is the same, leaf petals starting at a and sewing out at b. Sew in new threads for the other open petals. Make a stalk from the large flower to meet the one from the bud; reduce pairs if necessary. Continue it down to meet and join a stalk from the other flower which can be tied off at k and the leaf made afterwards to cover the threads. Finally work the tendrils, stamens and filling. These have been left as spaces so that there is a free choice.

BUTTERFLIES AND MOTHS

These make attractive lace motifs and have been a source of inspiration for centuries as they give plenty of scope for using filling stitches. Bodies can be plain or fancy and the wings can be divided in many different ways. Moths are only different to butterflies in that their antennae are shorter and fatter and their wings shorter in depth. Begin always with the body as the wings join and cross over it quite frequently. This eliminates too many sewings and tied off threads.

Body (a)

Begin at the antennae, making a stem stitch from a and b to the head. Put in a gimp thread through these threads and use them to make the head. Have a foot on both sides crossing the gimp over and back to mark the divisions of head, thorax and abdomen. It will be necessary to increase pairs for the abdomen and this can be made more interesting by putting a twisted vein in the centre. Decrease to the minimal number of pairs at the bottom and tie

these threads with the weavers to form a tuft. This can either be sewn to the back of the abdomen or the threads can be woven in to the abdomen for neatness.

Body (b)

This is worked as body (a) but has a wide vein to the upper body. More threads will be needed as it is much wider, therefore increase to 14 or 15 pairs by the time a is reached. Leave out two pairs at a, b, c and d to work the open second body, gradually reducing pairs by leaving a pair out at e and f, to finish with three pairs at the bottom of the first body. These will be used to join the lower area. Work a braid from ab and cd, twist the pairs from e, f and g and take them into the braid as they are reached and as indicated in the diagram. Reduce the number of pairs gradually and join the two braids at h and finish off at i as in body (a).

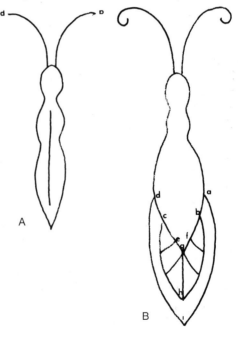

Diagram 68 A & B Butterfly bodies

Body (c)

This is a more ornate curved body and the antennae are worked last. Start at the top of the head with two pairs on a, b and c in a row. Work across all the pairs and add a foot on either side; increase rapidly to form the rounded top. From d to e is a raised surface petal, so add two pairs on the pin d and work through them as they are reached. Make a petal to extend to c and pin it in place. Work the thorax over the top of this petal absorbing the petal pair as they are reached. Reduce the number of pairs as necessary at the beginning of the abdomen and cross the gimp thread at the indents. This body can have the raised petal in a different colour by working through it once after e and then cutting the threads out. If they are left in it will give a stripe down the body; this is optional. It looks quite attractive with a very thick thread as a gimp. Thin cord is also effective, but in this case do not cross them at the indents, just pull up tightly. Finish the abdomen as before. The antennae are added afterwards to give the impression of the large eye. Begin at f with a stem stitch, curling the tip and sewing in to the head at g and j and in to itself at h and i. Finish off as neatly as possible at k.

Body (d)

This has moth antennae which are petal formations from a and b to the head. As they join the head at the side, three pairs need adding at c before the head is started. The thorax can be left plain with a vein in the centre but the diagram shows an open area. This is worked by increasing the pairs to 11 at d, dividing and leaving one pair hanging at d. Work both sides simultaneously leaving a pair out at e and f. At the same time begin the centre

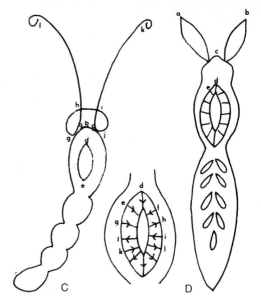

Diagram 68   C & D Butterfly bodies

filling just below d with the pairs from d, e and f. Work in cloth stitch bringing in a pair from g on one side and out into h on the other side braid. This goes through the cloth stitch centre. It is brought in again at i and out at j and in at k and out at l. Finish at the bottom as at the start with three pairs left to go out at the base. Join the two braids again and work the abdomen. This has a number of raised petals on the surface and will need the threads to do this, therefore increase to 16 or 18 pairs and work the petals, pinning them in position and working over them. They are staggered and another set begun before the completion of the first set, hence the need for a sufficient number of threads. Reduce the pairs gradually after the last petal has begun.

Any of these bodies can be used with the various wing shapes, but they will have to be enlarged proportionately. The wings are symmetrical so the other side is the same as the one drawn in the diagram.

Diagram 69   Butterfly wings

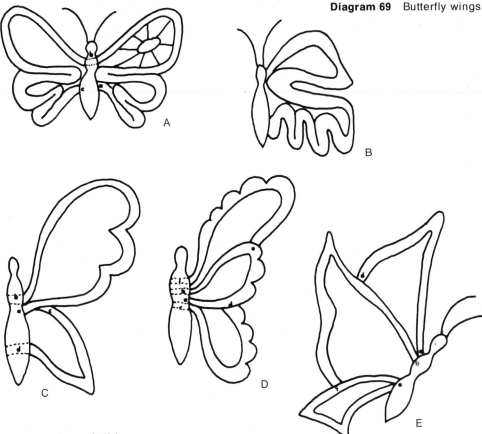

Wing (a) and (b)

These are formed by a continuous braid which begins at a, crosses the body with sewings at b and sews out finally opposite a at c. Wing (a) has a Bedfordshire spider as a filling but wing (b) does not require one.

Wing (c)

This is again a braid, beginning at a, crossing the body at b for the other upper wing. Sew in pairs at c crossing the body at d for the opposite lower wing, sewing out finally at e opposite to c. Do not forget to sew in each time the body is crossed.

Wing (d)

This is formed by an indented braid and a gimp thread will be needed as in the flower petals. Make the centre wing first, starting at a, crossing the body at b for the opposite side. Cross the body again at c for the lower wing, tying out at d. Sew in the pairs again at e, cross the body at f and tie off into e on the opposite side. This will leave one lower wing to be completed by sewing pairs in at d and out at c. There are now six spaces in which to put fillings.

Wing (e)

This is a side view; the body is worked in the same way but the position of the antennae is slightly changed. Work the bottom wing first, carrying the threads along the back to sew in at b for the second wing which sews out at c. Sew in again at d and finally out at e.

53

Moth Wing

This is a moth wing that begins at a, crosses the body at b, works the opposite wing, crosses the body again at b and completes the lower wing. Sew in to the upper wing several times as it is touched at c and sew out finally at d. The other lower wing is sewn in again at b on the opposite side and out at d as before. If preferred, the upper body only need be made.

Filling a multiple space

The moth has a suggested filling and it is useful to be able to keep all the threads in use throughout the working of all the areas to be filled. This eliminates too many tyings and too many knots which make the motif weak. All fillings for multiple areas can be organised in this way if careful attention is made to their positioning. The threads need to be angled so that they will do this.

Begin by sewing in threads to make the Maltese petals on the top wing. Sew in the two pairs for the stalk near the body and make the plaits and windmill joins through all the petals.

Divide the plait at the end into two twists and sew in at e. The petal at f is sewn in and plaits down to the body, sewing in at g and carrying the threads over for the stalk below at h. The second row of petals are now changed to plaits for the next row. Sew in another two pairs at i and plait down with windmill joins to j. Sew out the petal plait and leave for the filling below; take the threads from the plait to k and sew in, plaiting up to l. Take the threads and sew them into m and plait down to n; take the threads over to the flower filling for a petal. The other threads can now cross over for the rest of the flower petals and the leaves of the lower wing. Sew out the stalk at o and take the threads from the lower wing leaves out of the body in plaits at p, q and r over to the body. They can be sewn out here, or at p, q and r, or taken across the body for the opposite wing which would then have to be worked in reverse, lower wing first.

To make a flower centre

When a flower shape is made using

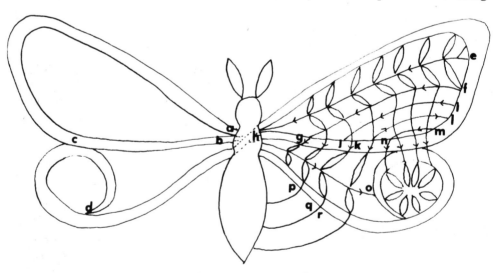

Diagram 70   Moth wing showing the working of a continuous filling

Maltese leaves a small, neat crossing of threads must be made. When the four petals are complete there will be eight pairs. As in a windmill join, treat each pair as one bobbin. Make a half stitch with the centre four pairs. Make a half stitch with the right hand four pairs and again with the left hand four. Make another half stitch with the centre four pairs and pin to the centre. Make a whole stitch with the centre four pairs, then take the right hand four pairs and cross the centre pair of these left over right. Take the left hand four pairs and cross the centre pair left over right. The petals can now be made for the lower part of the flower.

Flying Butterfly

This example shows how a butterfly need not be completely symmetrical if it is in flight; it is worked in the same way, using the curved body. Make the centre wing first on both sides, crossing the body as before. A second

Diagram 71 Butterfly in flight, non-symmetrical

crossing will enable the one lower wing to be completed; this divides at c and joins at d, sewing in to e. The second opposite lower wing is sewn in at f and sewn out in a wide area at g. The top wing has a series of surface petals and is started at h, crosses the body and is sewn out at i. The braid of this top wing will need more threads

Fig. 26 Flying butterfly in cream silk with gold. Thick gold gimp used on the body and gold surface petals on the upper wing, gold picot edge

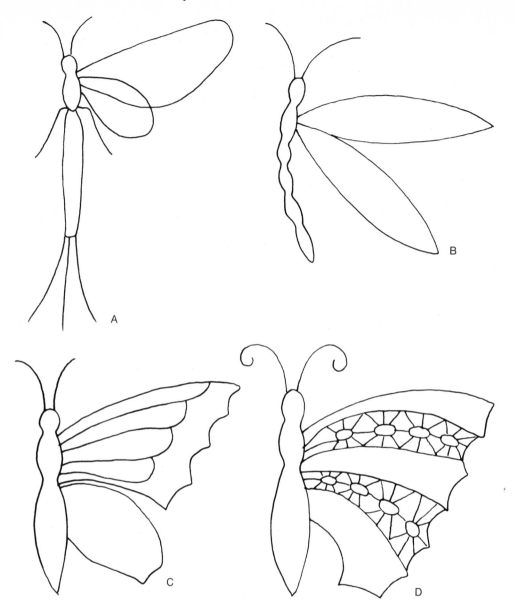

Diagram 72 A selection of butterflies and dragonflies

as it widens and to cope with the raised petals. It looks attractive with a picot edge to the lower wing. Both this edge and the raised petals can be done in a different colour.

There are several other forms of butterfly with a variety of wings, each of which would be worked separately as a series of braids with fillings in between. Diagram 72(b) could have its wings worked as leaf shapes in half stitch or with veins or holes. Diagram 72(c) could have the lines that form the veining worked by weaving a gimp thread through a mesh filling.

56

Fig. 26 shows the flying butterfly worked in cream silk with gold raised tallies and a thick gold thread used as a gimp round the body. Fig. 27 is a panel of butterflies designed by Elena Holeczyova using many different forms of decorated braid, held together with a mesh background and in several different colours.

BIRDS

The main technique for making birds is in the structure of the wings. The body of a bird requires dividing into suitable sections, of a size convenient to work, and each section is joined to the next with sewings. Wings are formed from a continuous braid, turning and sewing to itself, and the shape

Fig. 27 A panel of butterflies designed by Elena Holeczyova and worked in fine wool violet, grey, green and black with touches of gold. 126 × 166cm (50 × 65in)

depends on the position of the bird, whether static or in flight.

Swan (a)

This shows a simple technique for the body, formed from a continuous braid with a foot on both sides. It turns and is increased as becomes necessary.

Begin at a with five pairs and increase from b to eleven pairs. Change to half stitch at c and sew in and tie off at d.

The wing is a continuous braid, starting at a with five pairs and increasing to nine pairs until b is reached. Begin at b to increase to fifteen

57

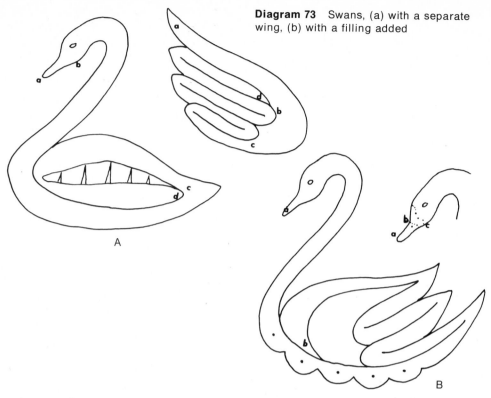

Diagram 73 Swans, (a) with a separate wing, (b) with a filling added

pairs on the outside curve and decrease gradually to seven pairs at c. Sew out finally at d. Wings look more attractive if they are worked in alternating whole and half stitch, one side of the feather is solid and the other more open. If two bodies and two wings are made, this makes an attractive mobile; the wings are sewn on afterwards to give a three dimensional appearance.

Swan (b)

This has no extra wing but is a continuous braid with a filling added afterwards. The braid is indented at the swan base and therefore needs a gimp thread on either side. It has a decoration of holes at the position of the marked dots.

Begin at the beak a and sew out finally at b; these threads can be used to make the filling which needs to be something close with a texture.

Swans are usually white or black but they can be given a coloured beak. Start at a with three pairs of orange and one pair white. Use the white pair as weaver throughout with no foot. Work to b and throw out one pair of orange to the back of the work and replace it with a black pair introduced in the centre of the work on a pin as in the diagram. Repeat this until all the orange are replaced by black, still using the white pair as weavers. At c the black need to be replaced by white and these are placed on the three holes marked, as well as on the outside edges. At this point increase as in swan (a) and add a foot to both sides. If colours are subtracted and added in this way with a continuous weaver the changeover will be gradual and the cloth stitch remains quite firm.

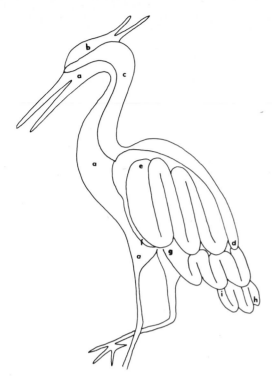

Diagram 74 Heron

ideas can be found in bird books. Sections are worked in order a, b, c, d to e, then f through g, h to i. Piece j is worked as a new piece with its beginning at h, sewing out into the tail.

The under body k is superimposed so that the feathers will lie over it and is worked on the dotted lines from the tail end. Sewings can be made at intervals to hold the pieces together. The feet l and m are worked last from the toe, sewing in to the body.

Birds in Flight

The following show the treatment of different wings in flight. All are continuous braids but the arrangement is different. Begin at a and sew out at b. You will notice that the tail can be treated in the same way as a continuation of the body working from c to d.

Diagram 75 Cockerel

Heron

The body is broken up into workable sizes, beak and underparts with one leg a, head feathers b, back c, and three sets of wings and tail. They should be worked in order, a, b, and c. The pairs are left hanging at d for the under wing. The top wing works from e to f where it is sewn out and the hanging pairs at d work to g and sew out. The tail starts at h and sews out at i. Finally the second leg is worked, starting at the claw and sewing in to the body at k. This bird looks well in colour; a is white with a yellow beak (a colour change is necessary), b is black, c and wing e to f are in shades of grey, as is the tail. Legs are yellow and a colour change will again be needed.

Cockerel

The cock is again divided into sections and looks very attractive in colour;

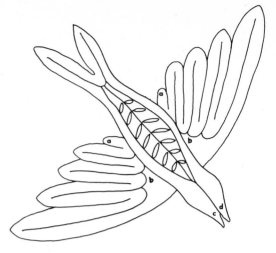

Diagram 76   Birds in flight

Three-dimensional Cockerel

This bird is worked in separate pieces and assembled like a soft toy, with a felt underbody which is wired. Two side bodies, one underbody gusset, two wings and two tails, four trousers and a feathered top are required.

Underbody
Begin at a, work in half stitch, increase to 20 pairs and make raised tallies where marked. Decrease to the minimum pairs at b. Finish off as for the

Fig. 28   Three-Dimensional cockerel in white linen thread

butterfly body.

Side body
Begin at b and keep the shaping by having the pin holes closer on the top edge. Shape carefully at the head and finish at a. Work in half stitch and increase to 25 pairs.

Wings
These are continuous braids, alternating half and whole stitch. Start at a and sew out at b.

Tail
Begin at a and divide the braid at b, working as for the open leaf, joining the braids again at c. Work a continuous braid from c following the diagram. A simple filling is inserted in the spaces in the feathers and each one can be different.

Trousers
These have raised tallies in the marked spots. Begin at a and work diagonally to b.

Head piece
Three small braids meeting and joining at the base.

To make up
Cut two side bodies and a gusset in white felt and oversew them together.

Diagram 77   Three-dimensional cockerel

Leave a hole on either side of the body at x for stuffing and to insert the wire. Stuff very lightly and place a U-shaped piece of wire through the body and out as legs (see diagram). Make the legs in silver or gold kid and enclose the wire, splaying out the wire and the feet. Make up the lace pieces, sewing them round the felt body; enclose the head feathers between the side body pieces. Place the trousers to cover the upper leg and sew into place. Wings and tail are sewn on to the body where desired and a triangle of kid forms the beak, sewn to the head. The eyes are beads or sequins. The model can then be stuck to a wooden plinth and covered by a transparent dome.

Diagram 78 Trees

TREES
Trees can be worked and mounted in several different ways and usually consist of a trunk with branches dividing into two and then into two again, and so on. The foliage is added afterwards in cloth stitch, half stitch or in any filling stitch.

Tree (a)
Its trunk and branches are worked as a braid, without a foot, which divides where necessary to form branches and twigs. Pairs will need adding as more branches form. The trunk and branches are worked first from bottom to top and the foliage worked afterwards from left to right in blocks, with the threads from one carried over to the next block in rope form. This looks better if the trunk and branches are worked in a textured knop thread and the foliage in a smooth, fine one.

Tree (b)
This has the same basic trunk and branch structure but has a net of filling stitches worked over the whole branch area. A small narrow foot can be worked round the filled area to hook the threads into, but it looks effective with threads added into the net as

62

needed (hanging a pair on the relevant pin). This forms a spiky surround which looks more realistic.

Tree (c)

The same basic structure but with a small amount of net between two or three branches giving a wintry look.

Tree (d)

The trunk structure is the same but the branches could be thinner. Individual leaves are added afterwards in woven form (see the section on leaves) or as Maltese leaves. This depends on the required size of the finished piece.

Tree (e)

A basic outline shape worked in half stitch starting at a and tying out at b. A filling of any kind is added afterwards. (See The Towers of Bruges, Fig. 40.)

Tree (f)

This is worked in the same way as the second leaf of the indented type and will form a Christmas tree.

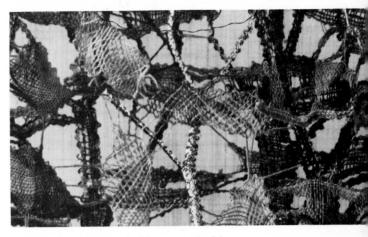

Fig. 29 Double panel of trees worked in 1-ply wool in autumn colours, used as a screen. It is suspended in a box frame but with no background, so that the panel can be viewed from both sides. Textured and smooth threads were used and worked in two separate pieces on a pillow. 78 × 45cm (31 × 18in)

Diagram 79 Mounting a three-dimensional tree within a box frame. Some branches are at the front, some half-way and some to the back. All are struck or tied through holes in the frame

Fig. 30 Black and white winter tree worked in wool and chenille, mounted in a perspex box frame as in diag. 79. 72 × 40cm (28 × 16in)

Trees can be mounted flat with a cloth background or between two sheets of perspex or glass to make a see-through panel, but are most effective if mounted in three-dimensional form. The trunk is attached to the base of a box-like frame and the branches are placed within the top and sides, some to the front, some to the centre and some to the back in the same way that a tree looks when growing. They can be attached with clear adhesive or with the threads pulled and tied through holes in the frame. Trees also look effective worked in two layers and mounted one behind the other as in fig. 29.

FIGURES AND ANIMALS

These need breaking down into workable parts for a variation in stitch, half, cloth, twisted cloth or a filling. This gives shading and interest both in the working and the finished look.

Squirrel

This is worked in a series of trails with sewings as in the bird's wing. Start at a on the forepaw and work up to b, turn as for a leaf and work down the back and up the tail, finishing at c. Begin the underbody at d and sew out at e; make the other paw and the two ears. A filling of any sort can be inserted in space f. Pairs will need adding as the width of the sections broaden.

Angel Fish

This has been divided into suitable areas for work. Areas a are in cloth stitch, b are twisted cloth to produce the ribbed effect of fins, c is half stitch and d are any filling stitches. The threads from the twisted cloth can be carried over for the filling from top fin to bottom fin and a hole can be added to make an eye.

The Madonna

As all pieces are worked on the wrong side, the areas that are uppermost need to be worked first. The baby's head is worked first and the threads left hanging to complete the body after the veil is finished. Work the Madonna's headband in gold starting at a and leaving the threads for the halo at b. Begin the shawl at c and work in half stitch up to b, cross the headband and work the top of the head to a, cross the headband and work down over the baby's head to d. There are a line of pin holes on the shawl which can be ignored, or you can divide the veil at the top point and work either side of the break, simultaneously meeting the weavers at each pin hole to form a curved line for the bend in the arm.

Fig. 31 Madonna worked in white and gold. 40 × 6cm (16 × 2in)

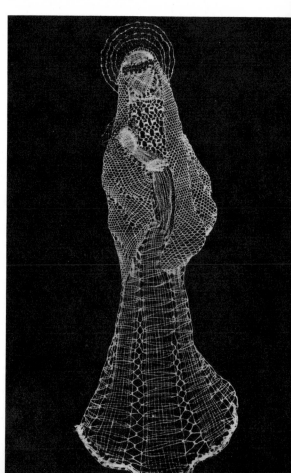

Diagram 80   Squirrel

Diagram 81   Angel fish

Diagram 82   Madonna

Continue the baby's body over the veil using a gold weaver. Tie the threads out on the shawl but some of the threads from d can be used to start the dress panels. Work the other piece of shawl e to f, and work the halo. This is worked in two circles, one within the other with sewings. The baby's halo is worked as one circle. The skirt is worked in three panels, i and j first, with threads from the shawl, in an open cloth stitch, leaving the threads at the bottom. Sew in pairs at k for the third panel, and after working it turn and make a narrow braid along the bottom from l to m. Keep the number of pairs constant but pick up the threads from the other panels, cutting out the second pair in from the edge, as a pair is absorbed from the dress. Darn the pairs out at m as neatly as possible.

Diagram 83 Jester, designed by Lia Baumeister-Jonker

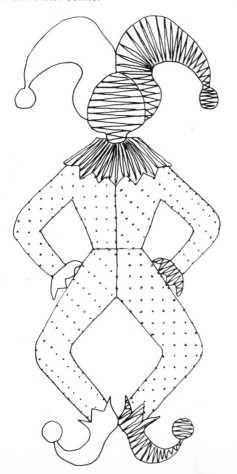

The face is worked in cloth stitch, as is the neck and sides g and h. The area n can now be filled with any stitch; lattice and cutwork has been used in fig. 31. This Madonna has been planned slightly differently to the diagram in that the hand and extra folds have been eliminated to simplify the working. The small areas between the dress folds are worked last and have a pair added at o, p, q and r which work a whole stitch and sew into the side panels at intervals.

The Jester
This can be worked in colour with hat in half stitch, face in twisted cloth, collar in alternating cloth and half stitch and the body in filling stitches.

Figures Designed by Martine Bruggeman
These have been drawn in as though they have been worked, so they are very easy to interpret. They consist of several different braids with other

Fig. 32 Jester in gold and silver threads designed and worked by Lia Baumeister-Jonker

stitches in between and are very open. They need backing with fabric and the place to begin is at a point of one of the main braids into which others are sewn.

Diagram 84 Girl with flowers, designed by Martine Bruggeman. Worked as a series of braids and edges, with threads carried through as much as possible

Diagram 85 Children with balloons,
designed by Martine Bruggeman

Diagram 86 Boy and girl, designed by
Martine Bruggeman

The following photographs of figures show different interpretations of the figure.

The Angel is a series of braids. The same number of threads are kept throughout but the twisting of passives and weavers makes the braid appear wider. Sewings are made at points of contact.

The bride is a figure in its simplest form, with cloth stitch and sewings with a fancy braid formation to make it more elaborate.

The Madonna with a bird is again simple in form. The figure has been divided into workable sections and half stitch and cloth stitch used.

Fig. 33 RIGHT and **Diagram 87** BELOW Angel in Schneeberg lace designed and worked by Lia Banmeister-fouker. Braids in cloth stitch, which change to twisted cloth when the braid widens.

Fig. 34 BELOW Bride, designed by Elena Holeczyova and worked in white and silver. 40 × 50cm (16 × 20in). Simple figure shape is given a bridal feel by by the flowered background

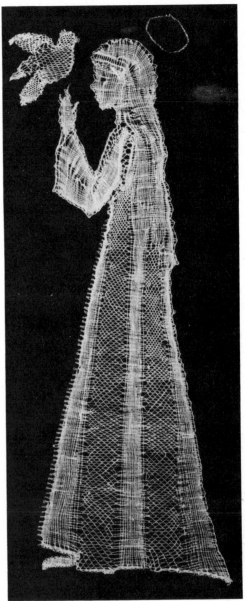

Fig. 36 ABOVE Madonna worked in one piece in white by Joan Tyler. Designed from a simple drawing with the effect captured by the use of cloth stitch and half stitch only

Fig. 35 LEFT The Wife of Robert Ingylton, Chancellor of the Exchequer to Edward IV in 1472, worked in lace by Judith Osborne from the brass rubbing. Worked in white and gold

Fig. 37 LEFT Virgo worked by Audrey Rae in cloth, twisted cloth and half stitch. No foot is used, giving a soft outline. This same figure has been used as one of the motifs on the Zodiac parasol but worked as a one piece lace. 12 × 12cm (5 × 5in)

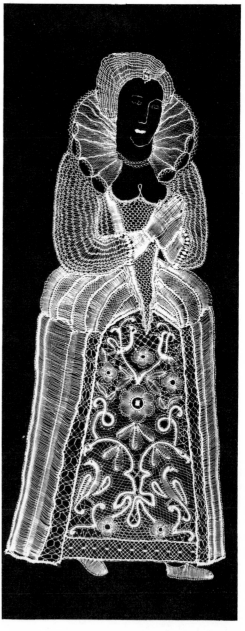

The seated figure has been worked in several sections with half stitch, cloth stitch and twisted cloth being used.

The brass rubbing is of a much more elaborate figure, with many different stitches, and the panel of the dress is in Bruges flower lace.

Buildings

These can be made interesting by the use of stitches as in the panel of roofs by Bridget Cook.

The Towers of Bruges are made in a fine thread and are worked by breaking the buildings into workable parts, with some of them solid and some of them open. The solid ones are broken by veining, lines of holes (windows), use of plaits and different use of stitches. The water is in half stitch braids

Fig. 38 RIGHT Figure from a brass rubbing has an elaborate dress using a wide variety of stitches. Designed and worked by Bridget Cook. 40 × 20cm (16 × 8in)

Fig. 39 ABOVE Panel of buildings worked and designed by Bridget Cook with a variety of stitches used to give texture

which change in width but keep the same number of threads; this makes it dense or open at intervals. The threads are sometimes left out to give dimension and perspective or to give a flowing effect to the water.

Fig. 40 BELOW The Towers of Bruges worked by The Animated Work Group for Modern Lace, Sisters Maricoles, Bruges Belgium. Made in fine thread by Honiton or Flemish techniques with use of cloth, twisted cloth, holes, windows, fillings and plaits to break up the buildings. Half stitch water and loose threads are placed skilfully to give the necessary dimension

Using Coloured Threads

To obtain a realistic picture using coloured threads the colour can be shaded and blended as one would do in embroidery. This can be done by working from a coloured picture or working directly over a painted drawing, adding or subtracting the colours as they appear. To work from a picture in this way the design may need reducing or enlarging as shown (diagram 105), working out in lace form and then painting or shading. Place tracing paper over the drawing to prevent the pencil coming off on to the threads and work over this. The colours can be added as explained in the swan beak; the weaver must remain constant.

When working in colour, it is all too easy to make everything in cloth stitch and to forget that lace is an open construction. Try to use filling stitches and twists to open it because it is this that makes lace so different from weaving; it will make it both more interesting to look at and to work. When using coloured threads there are a few points to observe.

1. As the cloth stitch parts are woven, it is very easy to create a tartan effect. This can be avoided by using a neutral or mid-tone as a weaver.

2. The weaver usually becomes the prominent colour and this can sometimes be used to advantage. For example, white passives can be used in a sleeve with a white weaver and changed to pink flesh for the hand merely by changing the weavers to pink.

3. When using filling stitches the colours will interchange. Plan the colours carefully to make the best use of this colour change.

4. Half stitch has a single weaver with its partner changing at every stitch. Allowance must be made for this.

5. Textured threads are too bulky to use as weavers; a thin thread is preferable and it will make the textured effect more obvious.

6. When dividing for branches on a tree in textured threads, a new thin weaver must be added at the break to make the new weaver on the other side.

7. A transparent thread is not satisfactory as a weaver; the thread is difficult to use and gives an undesirable sheen.

8. If a sheen is required as in a fish, the weaver can be in a very fine silver and it will not detract from the colour.

Diagram 88 Houses and trees, designed by Martine Bruggeman, worked in a series of decorative braids and stitches. As these join frequently the starting point can be optional. Carry the threads over as much as possible to avoid too many tyings

FIVE

The Development of Design

Lace in the future

Bobbin lace making is a way of producing a light, open construction that can support itself in the same way as a piece of woven fabric and design for lace should always exploit the particular qualities that are part of its technique. Lace is transparent, it can hold its shape and it can be composed of numerous stitch combinations that give it depth and shading. The purpose for which the construction is to be used controls to a certain extent the

design and the thread, but as with all art forms the technique and the fashion of the time must be considered.

The fashion in the late Renaissance was for heavy, sculptured decoration both in furniture, furnishings and dress. Lace design of this period was an extension of embroidery; the sty-

Fig. 41 Milanese lace showing scroll form with an uneven ground worked round the design. Spaces form part of the design

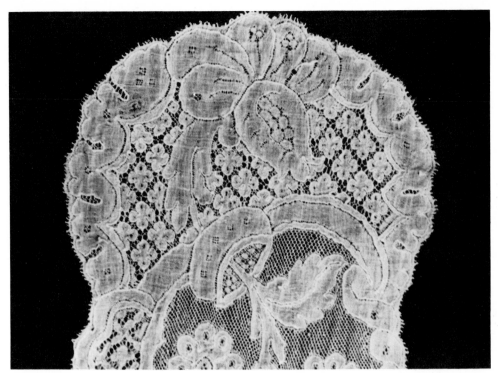

Fig. 42 Bottom of a Mechlin lappet showing the decoration used on the cloth stitch areas to give interest; varying size of filling gives shading

lised flowers and leaves of Venetian gros point closely resemble the crewel embroideries, and were heavily decorated with raised padded satin stitch. Bobbin lace at this time endeavoured to copy the needle-made designs and in some cases was quite heavy and coarse. Scrolling design was much in favour and variation in texture was created by the use of filling stitches and open spaces. Many of these early filling stitches bear a close resemblance to the needle-made ones. Much of this lace was used for church vestments and a bold design was necessary to be seen from a distance. The seventeenth century example of Milanese bobbin lace is 62cm (24in) deep and in a coarse linen thread. It was made in tape form with large holes created as the tape turned, and this has been used as part of the design.

The Baroque era was the age of fantasy, tall headdresses and coiffures with exotic embroideries. Lace was extremely popular as a rich decoration to dress for both men and women and it was in this period that the thread was exceptionally fine and lace design at its best. The position of the lace when worn made the design very important; edges needed to be of flowing repetition, head lappets needed an important design from top to bottom, and the cap back had the same design but planned within a triangular segment. Anything could be depicted in lace: birds, animals, people, flowers, butterflies or musical instruments.

The Mechlin lappet of this period in fig. 42 has a design of stylised flowers bursting from a cornucopia. The cloth stitch areas were decorated with holes and four pin buds to give

77

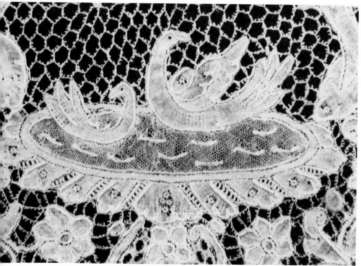

work on the feathers made them easier to work as well as giving them a dimension, and the size change of the filling stitches gave great scope to the designer. The use of plaited bars in some areas made very open parts possible and small raised bars have been added to the bird bath in fig. 44 to give waves. The birds in fig. 44 are very small, 1–2cm ($\frac{1}{2}$–$\frac{3}{4}$in), and were worked in incredibly fine thread, but the detail on each motif was of great importance to the overall appearance.

Even when enlarged these birds are beautiful, whereas in the panel of musicians each enlarged musician,

interest and an enormous variety of stitches had been developed to give the shaded areas. Lace became a work of art and as such was designed by artists.

The birds in fig. 43 are part of a Brussels lappet. The use of raised

figs 45 & 46, has a somewhat garish appearance. The lady at her spinet, fig. 45, has raised edges to give detail to hair and dress and the other musicians have detail to waistcoats, shoe trimmings and instruments. Each figure is about 3cm ($1\frac{1}{4}$in) high.

The Regency neo-classic period was simple and natural; flowers entwined with ribbons made in a fine thread gave a delicate pattern on a fine net background. It is interesting to note that machine net was available at this time.

By the Victorian era design was extremely varied, neo-gothic and neo-Elizabethan, and lace design followed the general trend. Throughout this period copies of all the old laces were available as well as some new flowing floral designs. Some of these were very realistic, with shading and three-dimensional petals to flowers and wings to birds.

The Chantilly panel in fig. 47 is a good example of lace techniques being used in an art form; the picture created resembles an etching. It is a river garden scene with birds, nets, lobster

Fig. 45 ABOVE Part of a panel of musicians with superimposed braid and raised edges used to give detail to the motifs

Fig. 46 BELOW Enlargement of the cellist in the musicians panel

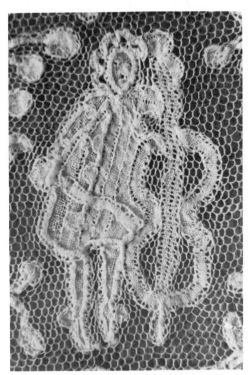

bins re-attached to work the centre.

When looking at old lace it becomes increasingly obvious that the finer the thread the more detailed the design can be, and the close link between design and technique is also apparent.

By the mid-nineteenth century design was influenced by the quickness of technique in competition with the machine, and heavier laces were becoming more popular. Up to this time lace designing had been done by artist specialists and lace workers interpreted the design; consequently designers were artists and workers were skilful technicians.

As machine made lace was cheaper and could be made quickly it was worn

Fig. 49 BELOW Musical instruments in Chantilly lace; half stitch and honeycomb with gimp threads

Fig. 48 ABOVE Detail of the water and rocks on the Chantilly panel. Worked in half stitch and twisted net, but with the water net pricked finer to give a little more contrast

pots and cages depicted in a watery environment with flowers, rushes and trees to surround. There is a great use of stitches to produce light and shade, with a profusion of gimp thread to form twigs, water ripples and birds' wings as well as to accentuate the lines on lobster pots and cages. There is a clever interpretation of a flowing waterfall using gimp threads and half stitch. The surrounding border has a variety of musical instruments in the corners, including banjos, trumpets and bagpipes. The whole panel is a one-piece lace but for convenience of working the surround was made as an edge with four corners and the bob-

Fig. 47 OPPOSITE Chantilly panel which resembles an etching. The detail in shading and representation seems to indicate that it was worked from an artist's drawing

extensively by more of the population. The hand-made variety was still expensive and it gradually became a dying art, especially in England. Old patterns were copied and recopied, usually to their detriment. Honiton lace became very poor in quality and design; some of the workers took designs from wallpaper and from worn prickings, and in Bedford the quickness of the new Maltese method produced a lace of inferior quality. Efforts were made to improve the situation, particularly with the 1851 and 1861 exhibitions and some of the best

nineteenth-century lace came at this time both by hand and machine. Schools of lace design were quite common on the continent and design was part of their course. France, Italy, Belgium, Germany and Spain still produced lace designers and many exhibited at the exhibitions. England too won several medals for lace but the names of many of these designers have been lost.

Some of the laces were worked from

Fig. 50 Deer panel designed by Thomas Lester, from the Cecil Higgins Art Gallery in Bedford

European designs but the Devon laces took a new lease of life, partly through royal patronage and the efforts of a Captain Marryat. New patterns were produced of insects, birds, flowers and other natural forms and these were worked in many of the Devon lace schools under the supervision of skilled lace teachers. Mention must be made of Mrs Treadwin, who made and designed many of the exhibition pieces.

Many medals were awarded to the Lester family of Bedford for unique lace design. Thomas Lester was the son of a firm of lace dealers and won medals in London 1851, 1862 and 1872, in Paris in 1867 and in Vienna in 1873. He combined fruit, flowers, leaves and animals to form the basis of his designs and the Bedfordshire/Maltese style for technique, producing a lace of unique character.

Each original design was drawn on grey card and carefully marked out to be made in lace, with pin holes marked at the intersection of threads. These were then made into prickings for production. His finest animal and bird pieces may have been worked for exhibition only and could have been done on his original drawing as there do not seem to be any prickings of these. Whether he worked these pieces himself or used his numerous skilled employees is not known, but from his drawings it seems that he could probably make bobbin lace. It is from these drawings that we can see the order of work and how he approached design. First a rough sketch of the design was made, then solid areas were marked, filling stitches were placed and finally the net or plaited background was put in.

Bobbin lace has not developed in the way that embroidery and weaving

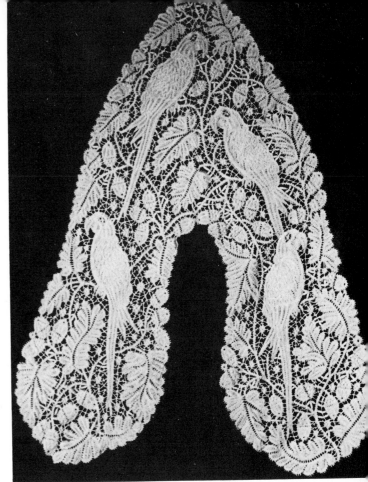

Fig. 51 Parrots in an oak tree designed by Thomas Lester, from the Cecil Higgins Art Gallery in Bedford

has, possibly because it is quite a long process to learn the techniques. It is only on the continent of Europe in the Textile Art colleges, particularly of Eastern Europe, that lace design and technique have been further developed since 1920 and it is seen there in a much more expressive and artistic form.

The problem that designing in lace has presented is the distinct difference between the artist designer and the skilled technician. The most expressive laces of the twentieth century have been produced by artists who were also skilled technicians and these are few.

83

To be contemporary lace needs to be of new design within traditional techniques, or new design with modern development of techniques. In all fields of life we no longer take traditional ideas for granted, we question them. The best contemporary laces have been made by adapting known techniques to create the desired effect. It must be stressed that a good working knowledge of lace is essential before one can design; one cannot adapt or break a rule if one does not know the reasons behind it.

Design in lace is affected by the two different techniques mentioned in the early part of this book. One piece laces are the most difficult because they are governed by their geometric form. Their solid areas and their background are worked simultaneously, so that all the bobbins are introduced at the beginning of the work and the same number remain throughout the piece. The design has to be worked out with this in mind and plotted mathematically in lace form before work can begin, plotting pin holes at the intersection of threads to support them. There is a relationship between mesh background and solid area which must be organised in making the design and choosing the thread to work it. An open mesh produces a light cloth stitch and a close mesh gives a dense one. Ground laces such as Torchon and Point ground have a mesh which is worked diagonally and cloth stitch pattern worked horizontally, which creates further difficulties.

The Bedfordshire/Maltese technique poses less problems as the plaited ground can be placed at any angle to suit the design; its only drawback is in the mathematics. One must have enough threads in the solid areas to allow for the passing in and out of the plaited bars.

Honiton or Flemish motif form is very much easier to design. The main cloth stitch areas can be worked first, adding and subtracting threads as they are needed to shape the design, increasing or decreasing the width. When the body is completed the bobbins are reintroduced and fillings and background are worked in sections. Russian tape lace is an even simpler form of this. Most of the contempory lace made today is worked by this method and it is the only way to control colour.

There are a few basic rules when planning a design in any art form, but as this is often a very personal thing it is often better to sketch a rough idea and analyse it afterwards. Most of us know when we like something we have drawn, but it is often more difficult to analyse why we do not like it and how to correct it.

1. Any design needs to be well balanced, with the weight equal on either side and not top or bottom heavy, but this does not necessitate symmetry. This is particularly important in lace as there is such a difference between solid cloth stitch, half stitch and open fillings. Great care is needed when planning these.

2. The eye needs to be held within the design; beware of strong lines which lead the eye away.

3. Focal points need the eye leading to them; curving lines often do this and they also create a feeling of movement.

4. When drawing from nature be careful to observe the lines of growth. Draw these first and fill in the detail afterwards.

5. A good design is usually pleasing from any angle, even upside down.

Diagram 89 Growth lines

6. Plan the use of filling stitches very carefully to avoid a 'busy' look which will detract from the original drawing. Think simple.

7. Consider the final use and cater for this when positioning the design. Central for panels, flowing for edges, and remember that a design which is the right way up on the front of a collar may be upside down at the back.

8. Consider the direction of working the design. Panels can be worked from top to bottom or side to side, and edges are worked continuously sideways, although the design may be at right angles so that it is the right way up when worn or mounted.

9. When planning any design in colour be aware of the light and shade, and plan where the light source is so that it is consistent. Light on the right means that the light threads are on the right and the dark threads on the left. Dark threads will be under a branch, light threads above. This is important in any drawing, even if it is only a single bird or flower. It will give the final result more depth and will look right.

Creating a Design

'Design' comes from the Latin – to mark out or plan. It is often thought of as a creative process, developing plans and patterns to form a coherent effective piece of work, pleasing to the eye. In all textile design the materials used and the technique govern the final appearance, so that with some experience one can begin to see what will work in lace techniques, adapting the ideas from a first drawing. Creativity relies on a sense of proportion, pattern and line, and ideas can come from other media. It need not be confined by tradition nor by an accepted style, but should be a personal expression or feeling formulated in a way that no other media can.

Ideas can come from many sources and with experience the worker can easily pick out ones that will be easy to interpret. Particularly suitable are children's drawings, drawings of natural subjects, trees, flowers, birds, and buildings. Drawings are easier to work from than photographs. Greetings cards can give inspiration as can drawings from primitive art; the secret is to keep it simple and to make a few sketches at first without much detail, just shape. Build up a collection of source references, illustrations, photographs, etc. with a sketch book. A designer in any field needs to cultivate an alert eye and an enquiring mind.

Drawing is fundamental to all kinds of art, it is a simple contact with life; the more one looks the more one sees, so the more one looks the better one draws. Draw simple things, do not make finished pictures. Do not worry if the drawing does not resemble the original. Gradually your eye will discover what are lace subjects.

Nature is a storehouse of visual imagery and one can create a feeling of design by contrasting one shape with another, one scale with another, line to mass, smooth to textured, tone to tone and sometimes colour to colour.

The first consideration is the purpose of the design; lampshade, picture, tablecloth, cushion, dress decoration, stole, shawl, etc. This will give the size, possible shape and probably the colour. Then the technique can be selected, whether one piece lace or in motif form or even a mixture of both, and finally the threads. One piece laces cannot be worked in several colours as the threads move about during working and cannot be controlled to form a coloured design. The colours can only remain as passives and a coloured weaver can only be used if it remains the same throughout the work. In lace designs the solid shapes are planned first, then the patterned areas and finally the background. This gives a working drawing from which a pricking can be made; never leave anything to chance. This is the most important part, and the more time spent on this to get an accurate design the easier will be the working. Sometimes fillings can be left till later, especially when trying a new stitch, but it is often better to practice a sample first before planning its use.

For example, it is decided that an owl would make a decorative picture. First draw out the size of frame, decide on the colour and threads. Draw a few owl shapes from a bird book and try to capture the essence of the owl: hunched body, large eyes and stumpy tail. Take one of the drawings and work on this; begin to interpret in lace but still in rough. Spider form-

ations make eyes, a Maltese leaf for a beak, wings and tail by the continuous braid method and some kind of spotted filling for the breast. Redraw these details, working out the braids, where the threads are coming from and going to, where to start and how each piece will link in to the next, carrying threads from one part to the next as much as possible. Go over the drawing as though working it and when all the points have been plotted, and only then, the actual working can begin.

This owl could be used alone and mounted on fabric or it could have an appropriate background. A few sketch-

Diagram 90 Owl pattern

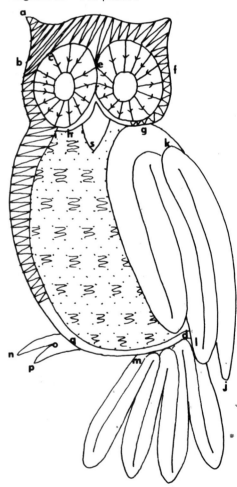

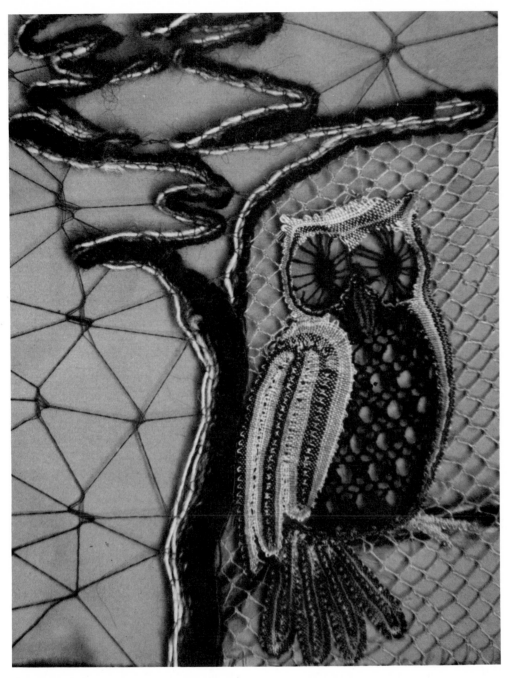

es could produce a tree with possibly a mesh to hold the owl in position and, if a foot is made round the picture to the size of the frame, it can be suspended.

Fig. 52 Owl in a wood, worked by Linda Moss in homespun wools and silk

87

Working the Design

The owl

Begin at a with three pairs and working with no foot; increase on either side until b is reached (14 pairs). Work to c and divide, working the left side of the head with five pairs and the right side with nine pairs.

Left side

Work five pairs round and under the body until d is reached; leave these hanging.

Right side

From c continue the top of the head; it will be easier to add and leave out four pairs at e for use when the eyes are worked later. Take out pairs as f is approached and work with four pairs to g. Take out one more pair to give three pairs to h, sew out and tie off at i.

Wing

Begin at j with three pairs and increase on either side until there are six pairs. Work a tightly curving braid, making sewings as the work progresses to k. Sew in and tie off.

Tail

Sew the five pairs left hanging at d in to the wing at l; work a tightly curving braid for the tail, sewing in where the braids touch and where they meet the body. Work until m is reached, sew in and tie off.

Claw

With three pairs at n work to o and leave, add three pairs at p and work to o. Join the six pairs and continue to q; sew in and tie off.

Eyes

Hang in 7 pairs above the eye openings as shown by the arrows and work the spider; seven pairs now have to be sewn in to the lower eye. One of the four pairs at e goes to the left eye, one

pair goes to the right and the two pairs that are left work a plait from e to r. A pair from the left eye crosses this plait and is used for the right eye. The plaited pair makes a tally from r to s to form the beak. These pairs can be left hanging to use in the breast filling.

Stomach

This is worked in cutwork and lattice filling as described earlier. Hang in two pairs above the relevant holes, sew in and add pairs as they are required. Sew in and tie out at the base.

Tree Background

Begin by pressing all the pins flat into the pillow and covering the owl to prevent the threads catching on the pins while the background is being worked. Start at a by laying six pairs lengthwise; add two pairs to make the weavers on either side. Work the left and right hand sides of the tree at the same time, meeting weavers at intervals to join it together. The two braids join at b and both sets make the trunk down to c. Sew into the owl body where it touches and leave long ends at the bottom to be sewn into the foot later.

Begin the foot at d with six pairs and two pairs for weavers as when starting the top of the tree. Work both sides simultaneously, adding pairs for the spider ground where shown. Sew in where necessary to the tree trunk and branches. Stop working the foot at e and f and begin the mesh ground surrounding the owl. The pairs from the spider ground at g, h and i can be sewn across to begin the torchon ground at j, k and l. Other pairs can be added as they are needed and these will be sewn in to the owl and absorbed into the foot where necessary. The foot can now be resumed on both sides, being worked simultaneously

Diagram 91 Background for the owl

with the mesh. It will sometimes be necessary to tie off threads into the owl and start them again somewhere else, but wherever possible carry them across the work. Remember that you are working on the wrong side; threads will not show through the cloth stitch areas but they will be visible through the filling. Both sets of foot pairs will meet and tie out and the threads from the tree trunk can now be tied out. The branch is worked from m to n over the claw.

Creating and interpreting a design in this way is working with all the familiar techniques applicable to all forms of bobbin lace, and putting them together to make the work easier, quicker and to give the desired effect. Most of the modern lace designs are

done in this way and working in sections enables one to use colour if so desired.

When making a picture think of a background as well; it makes the piece more interesting to look at and more interesting to work. For example, the angel fish in diagram 92 can have a seaweed background with shells, rocks and various types of weed interpreted.

Creating Dimension

Lace is usually two-dimensional, although many Victorian designs tried to give the impression of a third dimension in the use of stitch as in the Chantilly panel (Fig. 47), use of different threads as in Blonde lace and by adding extra petals to flowers and wings to birds.

Paintings and drawings achieve

Diagram 92   Angel fish with background

dimension by the use of colour and/or shading, making an otherwise flat piece appear rounded and in perspective. Egyptian tomb paintings made no attempt at perspective and figures appeared flat and unnatural.

Dimension can be given to lace in various ways.

1. By the subtle use of the different stitches.
2. By the use of gimp threads giving raised lines as in the Lester lace.
3. By using different weights of thread as in Blonde.
4. By adding extra wings or petals, or raised ribs and rolled threads.
5. By colour shading.
6. By making the lace itself dimensional in a box frame of wood or perspex.
7. By making a model as in the bird and the spray of flowers (figs 22 & 25).
8. By making a free-standing sculpture.

Modern lace does not have to be dimensional or make any attempt to appear dimensional; this is just one aspect of design and is merely a personal interpretation. This personal aspect in free lace design explores the whole spectrum of bobbin lacemaking in order to create an interesting and attractive piece which is individual. It is possible to design within the limitations of one particular form of English lace and these divide into Honiton (motif Form) and Point ground Torchon and Bedfordshire/Maltese (one piece laces).

Honiton

Design in Honiton is the same as in any free design except that it is worked on a much smaller scale and can be more detailed when a finer thread is used. It needs to be a pleasing combination of clothwork, raised work and fancy fillings which bring out the technique at its best. Spaces can be created within the design so that these fancy stitches can be used.

The width of the cloth stitch should normally be limited to 20 pairs and with this in mind either divide the section in two parts, create a space for a filling or give the cloth some form of embellishment such as veins, holes or raised spots. It is advisable to plot the course of the threads and arrange the design so that raised ribs or roped threads can carry from one section to another. This saves time and makes the work stronger. Too many tied off threads detract from the work and make the lace weak. Backgrounds can be added to many of the traditional

Fig. 53 Honiton cock, by Mrs Muzzlewhite

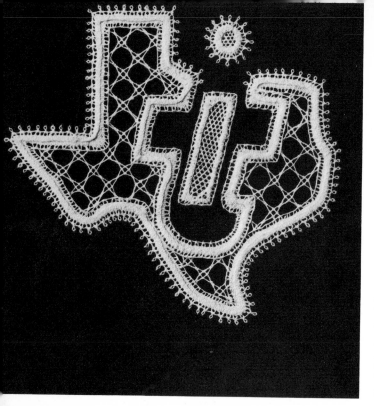

Fig. 54 Abstract Honiton used as the trade sign for Texas Instruments, designed and worked by Mrs Rutgers

Honiton motifs and all the design suggestions given in the first part of the book can be used if they are reduced in size. The owl and the fish would both make excellent Honiton designs.

One Piece Lace

Making one piece laces affords the opportunity of constructing a piece of transparent material which will stand alone, hold its shape and be reasonably strong. It need not be backed by material and therefore its transparency can be used for lampshades or see-through hangings, and its strength makes it suitable for dress decoration, table linen and soft furnishing. It is best made in one or two tones although textured threads can sometimes be used. These laces divide into three types, Torchon, Point ground (often referred to as Bucks) and Maltese (often referred to as Bedfordshire/Maltese). They each have their place but their design is planned differently.

The technique will control the designing to a certain extent and the positioning of the design is fundamental to the working of it. For instance, if one is working a handkerchief edge it is more usual for the design to flow along the edge, which is in fact the way it is worked, but if a length is for a drum lampshade it is still worked lengthwise, possibly of a width to cover the shade. The design need not be a flowing one but could be of buildings. Each building would have to be designed to be worked sideways. If, however, the lampshade was worked in panels, these would be worked from top to bottom and the design would have to be worked in this way. (See the design of a pagoda in torchon, diagram 94). The direction of working and the starting point is often a difficulty, especially when working someone else's design. When making one's own design this is planned right at the beginning and therefore presents no problem.

There are basically three shapes to consider: angular, curved and abstract. These are subdivided as follows.

Angular   squares, rectangles and triangles; parts of these form edges and corners.

Curved   rounds and ovals; parts of these are collars, fans, circular edges.

Abstract   irregular pieces with no regular form but still made in one piece.

There are various ways of working these shapes and the design can control the method or vice versa.

Squares are worked from top to bottom, side to side, diagonally or in four triangular segments.

92

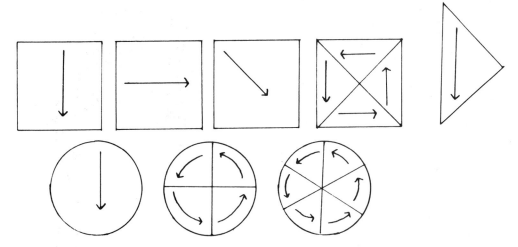

Rectangles are worked from top to bottom; edges are a series of rectangles changing direction at the corners.

Triangles are usually half a square and are worked from sharp corner to sharp corner.

Rounds are worked from top to bottom, side to side, in four segments at 90° or six segments at 60°.

Ovals are worked from top to bottom.

Abstracts are worked from top to bottom or side to side and usually have several possible starting points. There is no rule; it depends on the resemblance to a regular shape.

Any piece of ground lace will fit into the above categories and the design can be planned accordingly.

Designing for Torchon

This is a simple angular lace worked out on graph paper at 45°. It does not lend itself easily to curved shapes but to straight geometric. If one thinks of the designs for counted thread, blackwork or cross stitch these will also work in lace. There is a certain amount of freedom if one uses tallies, leaves and plaits within the ground but there are a few points that are important.

1. When planning cloth stitch areas

Diagram 93 directional ways of working shapes with grounds

and ground stitches, each pin hole should have a ground stitch coming in or out of it to avoid a distorted hole. This can be overcome by working the cloth stitch close or incorporating the distorting hole into the design.

2. There must always be enough threads in the cloth or half stitch areas to make them dense enough for the design to stand out. Extra pairs can be added for this purpose and removed before the ground starts again.

3. There is an optimum size of cloth stitch which looks neat and is workable; break the larger areas into smaller ones and introduce filling stitches or embellishments such as veins, holes or raised spots.

4. Scandinavian countries use a gimp thread to add interest, often using it alone, weaving in and out of the ground. When it is used to surround a shape it often gives that angular shape an illusion of roundness.

5. Remember the direction of working and draw the design accordingly. Angular figures work well in Torchon, particularly the cut-out paper doll type. One can make use of

A

B

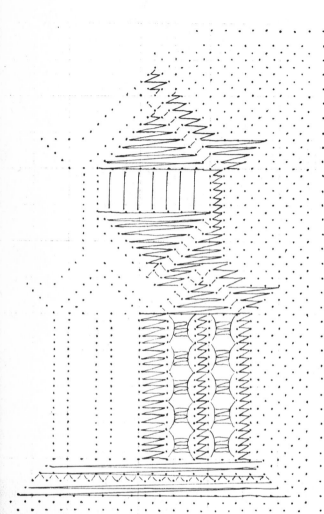

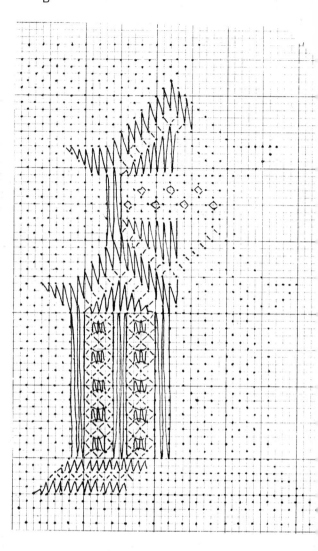

Diagram 94 (a) A pagoda in Torchon workable from top to bottom, divided into trails or triangles with tallies in the door openings

Diagram 94 (b) The same basic pagoda but planned to be worked sideways. Notice the change in direction of the tallies and the necessity of putting in a filling instead of bars at the top window; the threads are not available for making bars

the many stitch combinations for the dresses. Buildings are a very good subject as they are angular and only need breaking into suitable working areas with different stitches to give interest.

The two pagoda examples in diagram 94 show the difference in design between working lengthwise and working from top to bottom.

The fan shows (fig. 55) the use of

94

Fig. 55 Fan worked in Torchon on circular graph paper. A variety of stitches were used for the dresses. Notice the close ground at the base and the more open top; the design has catered for this particular fault that occurs when using circular graph

Fig. 56 Tree in Torchon for use on a lampshade, very straight and angular

stitches on the dresses and has been worked out on circular graph paper. This gives a dense ground at the base opening out at the top; the design was planned with this in mind.

Two trees (figs 56 & 57) were designed for a lampshade; one is very straight and angular, the other is much freer with leaves and plaits. The same fence in Rose ground has been used as the border.

Fig. 57 Tree in Torchon but with a much freer interpretation by using leaves and plaits. Rose ground is used as the fence throughout

Preparation for Torchon design

1. Draw out the shape of the desired piece and decide on the threads.

2. Choose the graph paper grid suitable for the thread.

3. Plot the ground over the whole piece; it is useful to have one or two photocopies of this to work on.

4. Sketch in the design; this can be original or a tracing fitting into the ground hole markings.

5. Go over the design as though working it, filling in any other dots that are necessary.

6. Trace off the design for working and either work directly from this, mounting it on firm card or pricking it out on to card.

Point Ground Design

The essential difference between Torchon and Point Ground is in the angle of the ground to the cloth stitch, and this can be anything between 55° and 70°. This angle makes a net that is rounder, enabling one to be much freer in design as it accommodates to curved shapes as well as to straight lines. It is usually worked with a very fine thread on a small grid and enables the design to be more detailed.

Preparation for Point Ground design

1. Draw out the shape of the finished piece.

2. Select thread and grid size.

3. Draw in the solid parts of the design within the selected shape, planning the open areas and the outer edge. Trace off on to thick tracing paper. (Do not use greaseproof paper. It is too flimsy and tears too easily.)

4. Plan the filling stitches in balanced areas but do not fill in.

5. Fill in the ground dots at the correct angle to the cloth area or foot side, marking them in where they contact the cloth.

Diagram 95 Crab in point ground partially marked in to show the order of procedure and showing the different treatment of edges in plaits with picots or just picots

6. Mark in the filling stitches at the same angle so that they follow through.

7. Go over the design as though working it and fill in further dots where necessary. An accomplished worker can probably do this as it is worked.

8. Prick and mark out on card or work straight from the tracing supported on card. The thick architect's tracing paper is most suitable as it is tough and does not tear with the pins. Working direct eliminates the time spent in pricking and marking out and reduces the error. Working over it on blue card is comparable with the vellum used by our ancestors.

The crab design (diagram 95) is planned within a circle and is one of 12 signs of the Zodiac worked on a parasol cover (fig. 58). The pricking is shown with different edges planned.

Edges and corners

Point ground edges are straightforward but corners cause problems because the ground will not make a 90° corner. There is always a small space where the two edges meet, and point ground distorts if the working direc-

Fig. 58 Zodiac parasol cover worked in two shades of cream silk. Honiton and Point ground techniques used, and worked in sections. Shading in mayflower filling to a honeycomb ground, various fillings used in the motifs with lattice and cutwork in the star

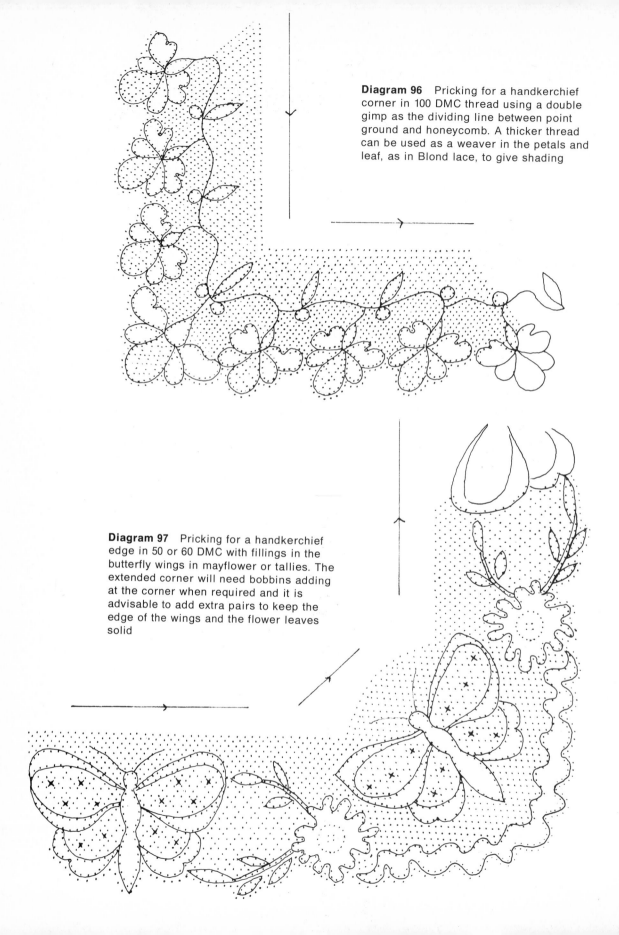

Diagram 96 Pricking for a handkerchief corner in 100 DMC thread using a double gimp as the dividing line between point ground and honeycomb. A thicker thread can be used as a weaver in the petals and leaf, as in Blond lace, to give shading

Diagram 97 Pricking for a handkerchief edge in 50 or 60 DMC with fillings in the butterfly wings in mayflower or tallies. The extended corner will need bobbins adding at the corner when required and it is advisable to add extra pairs to keep the edge of the wings and the flower leaves solid

tion is changed. This can be overcome by making a solid area somewhere on this corner so that the ground comes in to it and out on the other side. An example of this is given in the pricking of an edge with a floral design (diagram 96). The other alternative is to make a corner that is pricked at an angle to the corner point and the design planned so that the corner is cut off from the edge. The butterfly edge (diagram 97) is designed in this way.

The corner of this design can be worked on its own for the points on a collar or handkerchief. The other butterfly corner (diagram 98) is an example of a corner with the ground coming into and out of a cloth stitch body so that there is no angle change.

Designing a repetitive pattern
Any repetitive design can be worked

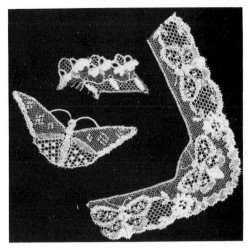

Fig. 59 Floral edge, butterfly edge and butterfly corner in point ground

as a circle in sections or as a circular edge by the following method.

1. Take a shape or several shapes, either original or from old lace or prickings. When choosing this shape think of its potential as a repetitive pattern on a desired finished piece. The illustrated shape (diagram 100) has possibilities of joining to itself and thus creating spaces between with an already slightly circular outer edge. It must be workable in a sideways direction.

2. Use isometric paper which is

Diagram 98 Butterfly corner begun at tip A, with the threads gradually decreased by B where they can be darned away or bunched together. The edges of the wings can be in honeycomb buds or solid rings. Picots are made on the outer edge and a foot on the other

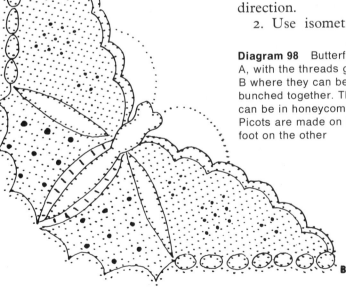

99

Diagram 99 LEFT Motif for use as a repeat pattern

marked at 60° and divide the circle into six segments by marking the lines in from the graph paper which lead from a central honeycomb stitch.

3. Position the motif centrally on the markings until their outer edges touch; lightly fill in the circular shape for guidance.

4. Line up the markings to the lines of the graph paper, pivoting on the central honeycomb, and work out how

Diagram 100 Motif placed centrally to the segment lines drawn from the central honeycomb

the ground can change, how to block in the spaces and any other details necessary. When the idea satisfies, fill in the ground dots. Any honeycomb holes must follow the direction of the ground.

5. Mark in any dots that meet the motif and then go over the pattern as though working it, filling in any further details.

Diagram 101 ABOVE One-sixth of the circular motif marked out

One segment is shown already planned with honeycomb holes in the ground to give interest and any gaps closed with a small ring. Six of these segments are required to make the circle.

The most convenient place to start the mat is in the centre of the motif a to b. The join will be less conspicuous if a twist is put in the centre of each motif every time, which will help its appearance.

This same motif can be spaced out to form a circular edge. Plan so that it fits equally round the circle. Use circular graph paper and this will help as one can use the radii as guides. This time there will be a bigger gap between motifs which will need bridging, and if it is being attached to a linen middle it will need a foot or other edge at the base. The ground for this can be pricked from circular graph paper and this makes it easier to work. (See the grids at the end of the book.)

Diagram 102 BELOW Motif arranged in a circular pattern

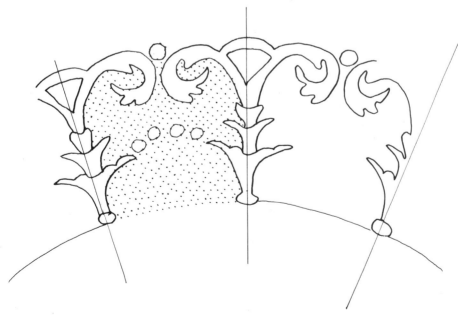

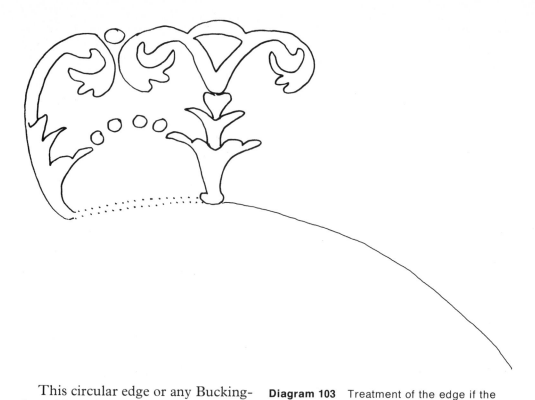

Diagram 103 Treatment of the edge if the circular pattern is used for a collar

This circular edge or any Buckinghamshire edge can be made circular by pricking on this paper and spacing out the design. A half-circle forms the basis for a fan leaf or a collar, and when designing these, lower edges and sides have to be planned. The illustrated one (diagram 103) is simply a matter of curving the first motif. The main disadvantage of circular graph paper is that the number of bobbins required is greater. The line of ground is an arc of the circle; this does not matter on a narrow edge, but if it is for a wide fan another method is probably better. This can be done by dividing the fan into segments, each separated from the other, and pricking these at different angles to each other.

The deer mat (fig. 60) was worked in this way. Each motif is divided from the next by a tree and roots. The threads from the ground are collected each time in the tree and the change in

the direction occurs when they are dropped out on the other side. The angle is worked out for each segment in a circular rotation.

Bedfordshire/Maltese

Designing in this follows the same preparation as for point ground, and as plaits are used instead of twisted threads there are usually more threads available for the solid parts. (The peacock's tail in fig. 102 has been worked out on circular graph paper using the radii as a guide to the positioning of the Bedfordshire spiders.) Thomas Lester's lace shows how effective design is in this form. He made complete pictures, such as deer in a wood or birds in an oak tree. The ground often had extra embellish-

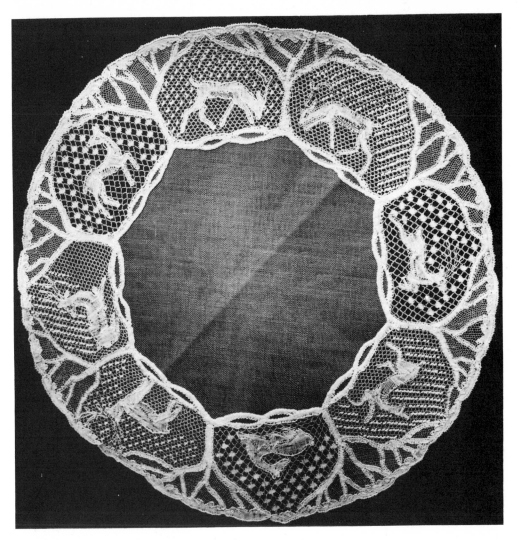

Fig. 60 A Year in the Life of a Deer, 42cm (16½in) diameter. Circular mat with each section pricked at a different angle. Tallies or mayflower used as shading to the honeycomb

ments and Maltese leaves to give more interest to the plaited background. The technique for giving texture to the motifs can be seen in fig. 62 where several small areas are worked simultaneously, weavers meeting through the gimp and returning to their own side. On a wide area such as the deer, the working must have been very difficult. This same method was applied to leaves and birds' wings and tails; this gave a very lined look to his design which added both dimension and texture.

The design for a Bedfordshire edge (diagram 104) is taken from Thomas Lester's sketch book and it shows how the design is built, how the threads are calculated and how the veins in leaves are marked. There is no detail to the flower filling and hardly any pricking dots have been filled in. This would have been done at the next stage.

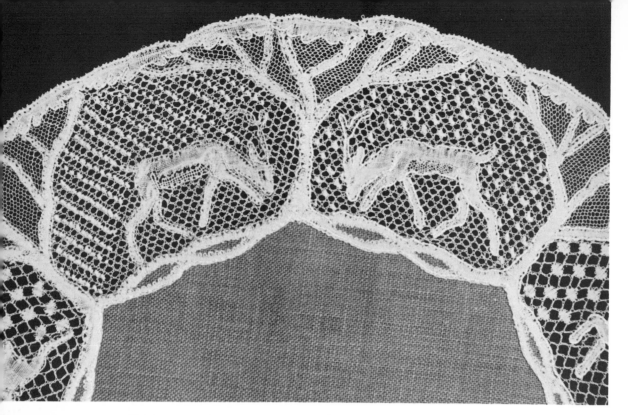

Fig. 61 ABOVE Detail of A Year in the Life of a Deer

Fig. 62 BELOW Detail of Bedfordshire lace from a Thomas Lester panel showing use of gimp and meeting of weavers to give detail

Diagram 104   Design for a Bedfordshire
edge by Thomas Lester partially pricked

Fig. 63   BELOW Detail of parrot panel by
Thomas Lester showing working of tail
feathers and leaves. Raised petals are on
the small rounds in the filling with the
occasional petal to fill in a space

LACE IN THE FUTURE

Bobbin lacemaking has been revived and is growing fast as a craft worldwide. In many countries it is worked in traditional patterns and forms part of their tourist industry. Some countries encourage a more modern approach, particularly in Belgium, France and Czechoslovakia, while others such as Holland, America, Sweden and Great Britain have several lace makers who have developed their own ideas in a modern form. All over the world, especially in the developed industrial parts, there is a nostalgic looking back at the past, a rebellion against mass production. Art

Fig. 64 Modern interpretation of Bedfordshire lace designed and worked by Joyce Scales from a silhouette of two old lacemakers in Abington Museum

has begun to pay more attention to detail; there is much more stitchery to be seen in embroidery and more visual representation in painting, more concentration on technique. Lace is a skilled technique with plenty of scope for designing within its limitations as one can see from past designs. In order to progress it needs to be taught and developed within the Textile Art Colleges where design is the basis of all textile work. Any design course is valuable to lace makers and can be adapted to the technique.

Marie Vankova Kuchynkova, an artist designer in Czechoslovakia, has said of contemporary lace that 'to man in his technical world, lace can become something extraordinarily beautiful and precious, which would help his festive hours and increase his awareness. Lace on a dress can be compared to precious jewellery, inherited from one generation to another.' We should perhaps be working towards this end, to create in bobbin lace works of art that will be appreciated by our great, great grandchildren in the same way that antique lace is appreciated now.

There are three aims in keeping lacemaking alive:
1. To safeguard and preserve the intricate techniques.
2. To develop it as a modern textile form.
3. To maintain a sociological phenomenon in traditional regions.

There are many societies which help to promote these aims by providing classes for technique and newsletters or magazines to exchange ideas.

Fig 65 A simple roundabout worked in coloured threads by The Animated Work Group for Modern lace, Sisters Maricoles, Bruges, Belgium

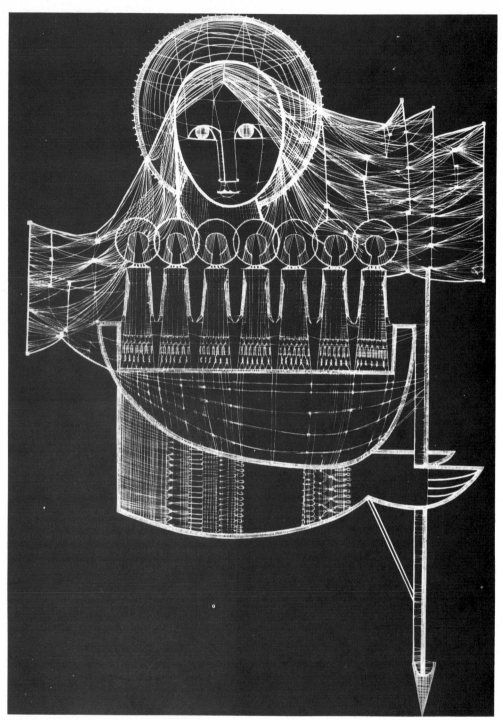

Fig. 66 Saint Ursula, by The Animated Work Group for Modern lace, Sisters Maricoles, Belgium. 55 × 40cm (22 × 16in).

There is an interesting use of loose threads to create the effect

The Lace Guild of Great Britain and the International Old Lacers of America both do this and they have members all over the world who in turn form groups and societies in other parts. Most classes in America are privately run, where a group get together and work under the guidance of a teacher. In Great Britain some classes are private, some are organised by Local Authorities and there is a private Lace School in Devon. One of the main drawbacks is the lack of skilled teachers, for without these lace cannot move into the Art Colleges.

Progressive lace courses are held at the Kantcentrum in Bruges, Belgium, and design is part of the tuition. Anyone interested in learning can go there as a pupil and they run a six-year course to train teachers. There are classes available in many other towns in Belgium and they are helped by the Ministry of Education. They work both traditional and modern designs and areas of Belgium have once again become distinct in their style of contemporary work. Their method of tuition is very disciplined as they have to show competence in one form of lace before moving on to learn the next. They begin on Torchon, Russian Tape and Cluny and then progress to Bruges Flower lace and Duchesse (similar to Honiton). They finally graduate to the finer laces such as Binche and Chantilly or develop their technique in modern style. Design and experimentation is encouraged and there are several lace designers who give guidance, tuition and sometimes supply designs. The modern approach has been developing in Belgium over the past 50 years.

There has been a Lace school in Le Puy in southern France since the sixteenth century. The 'Initiation à la

Fig. 67 Horse heads, designed and worked at the Centre d'Initiation à la dentelle in Le Puy, France. A series of shaped braids in shades of blue and orange

dentelle', as it is called, offers similar courses, and progression is structured in a similar way with modern design being taught after the techniques are perfected. There have always been designers in the school and as fashions change they have kept pace with original work. Teachers are appointed by the school and they have a State certificate of aptitude. There is a National Workshop set up in Le Puy where bobbin lace is manufactured to order for dress and furnishing and this offers employment to the workers in the area.

Textile colleges in Czechoslovakia have been working and designing for lace and weaving for many years, and the works which have come from these have a much more artistic approach than anywhere else. There is a special studio for embroidery and lace at the

Fig. 68 ABOVE Harlequin, designed and worked at the Centre d'Initiation à la dentelle in Le Puy, France. Multi-coloured threads

Fig. 69 OPPOSITE Moscow Basilica, designed by Monsieur Michel Jourde and worked by the Centre d'Initiation à la dentelle in multi-coloured threads and gold. 33 × 25cm (13 × 10in)

School of Applied Arts in Prague which began in 1946. It has developed since to include weaving, needle and bobbin lace, applique, macrame and industrial lace for dress and curtains. The basis of all their textile activity is drawing, mostly from natural sources, animals, figures, flowers and buildings. They then work the drawings out for their own particular technique. They find a unity between the possibilities offered by the mixture of techniques and the use of colour and various threads in order to express their ideas. Sometimes the techniques conform so much that lace can look like weaving and weaving resemble lace. The course is long, for six years, but very exciting work can result from it.

These lace schools on the continent have always taught design or employed textile designers, whereas in Britain lace design has never been taught. British design was usually the work of talented individuals who produced detailed patterns for their workers; these patterns became traditional and their origin was lost. Many patterns came from the continent or were copied from continental laces. If we are to keep lacemaking alive and develop it to suit our modern way of life it needs to be looked at in a new way. Its domestic use, which is how it began, is no longer so desirable in our

Fig. 70 Ice Skaters, by Elena Holeczyova, simplified figures held together by only a few threads to keep them suspended within a frame

Fig. 71 Wedding Dance of the Bridesmaids, 208 × 196cm (82 × 77in). Worked in natural and magenta linen thread with gold and designed by Elena Holczyova. The feeling of movement is created by the use of circles and curved positions of the figures, the curving movement going from top to bottom. A very well-balanced design,

life style, but if it could be developed as an art form it could take its place with other textiles such as weaving and embroidery, which are already held in high regard. We must have no nostalgia for the past work of lacemakers but analyse its place in our environment, how best to use its versatility to create something beautiful and exquisite which can justify the time spent on its techniques.

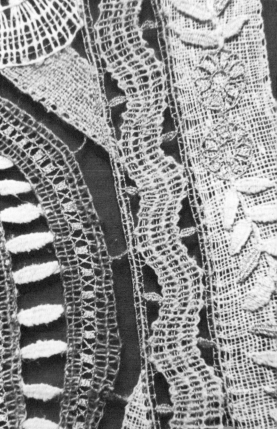

Fig. 72 Detail of the bridesmaid dress showing the use of surface petals and decorated braids. Each piece is worked separately and joined afterwards, and worked on a large roller

Fig. 73 Detail of another dress

Fig. 74 Detail of circles and flower
formations, and the treatment of the hand
and head-dress

Fig. 75 ABOVE Composition of Discs, designed by Elena Holeczyova. 157 × 157cm (62 × 62in). Worked in natural linen with gold. The open spaces between discs are an important part, forming an open transparent hanging which could be viewed from both sides

Fig. 77 FAR RIGHT The Medallions of Liptov (mountains in Slovakia), 80 × 350cm (31½ × 138in). Designed by Elena Holczyova and worked in natural linen. An interestingly designed wall hanging with different motifs arranged in circles

116

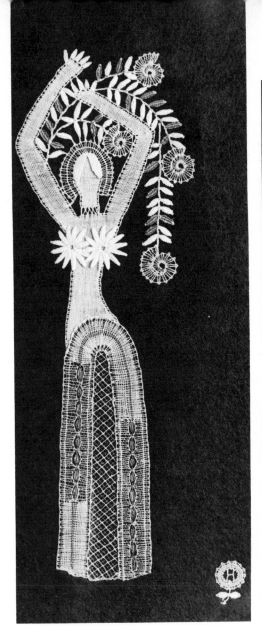

Fig. 76 ABOVE Flower girl, a figure in simplified form with the curve of body and flowers giving the feeling of movement 28 × 48cm (11 × 19in). The little flower at the base is the personal signature of the designer Elena Holeczyova. She is one of the leading designers in Czechoslovakia and has been designing for lace since 1945. Her interests are in theatrical design and her lace shows this and her interest in folk art and life. She has won many medals and prizes for her work

Fig. 78 ABOVE Lace miniature sculpture, 20 × 13 × 10cm (8 × 5 × 4in). Designed and worked by Marie Vankova Kuchynkova in white and natural flax with gold and silver lace in an interesting dimensional form, but still retaining transparency and a delicate quality

Fig. 79 NEAR RIGHT Dimensional waterfall suspended from the ceiling, worked in black and white flax and designed by Marie Vankova Kuchynkova, 6m × 80cm (19ft 8in × 31½in). It was exhibited at the Montreal Expo 1967 and is the property of the museum of lace in Vamberk, Czechoslovakia

Fig. 80 FAR RIGHT Lace designed by Marie Vankova Kuchynkova as an extension or continuation of the dress through removing the weft threads and using the remainder to work the lace. The lace then corresponds to the dress in colour and thread

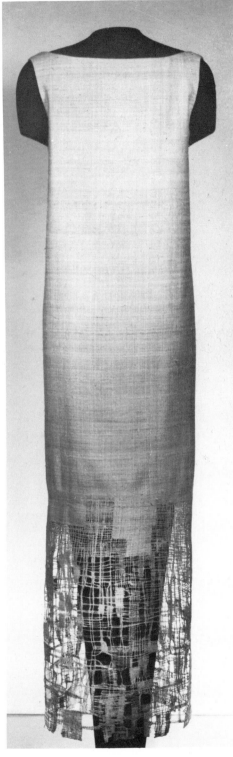

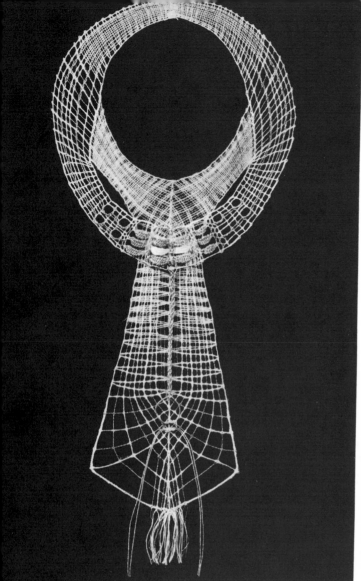

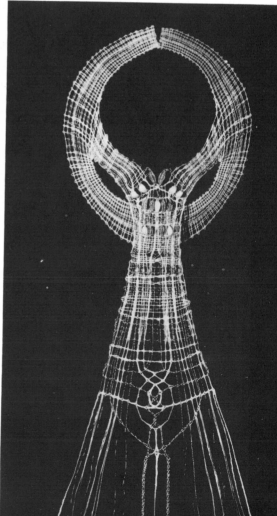

Fig. 81 LEFT Necklace designed and worked by Marie Vankova Kuchynkova in white linen and gold

Fig. 83 NEAR RIGHT Necklace designed by Marie Vankova Kuchynkova in gold, old gold and yellow threads with pearls as an integral part. It is worked in two transparent layers which combine to give a dimensional piece. Marie is Assistant Professor at the School of Applied Arts in Prague and she specialises in lace and embroidery. She works dimensionally, often over specially shaped pillows to mould the design. Her lace is sculptural but in classic form and is therefore timeless

Fig. 82 RIGHT Necklace designed and worked by Marie Vankova Kuchynkova in white and gold

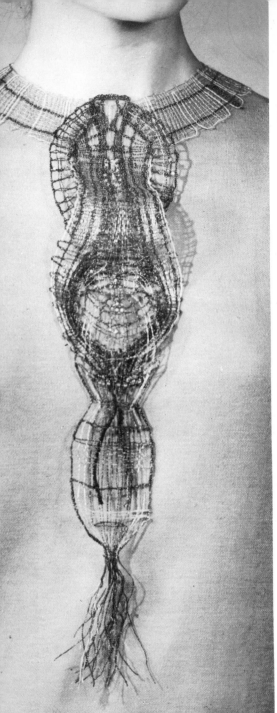

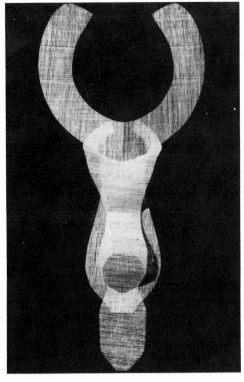

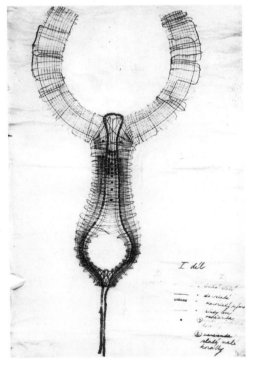

Fig. 84 TOP RIGHT Model of the necklace
(fig. 83) in two parts in buckram to get the
correct shape prior to working.

Fig. 85 BOTTOM RIGHT Lace outer part of
fig. 83 having been worked on a pillow

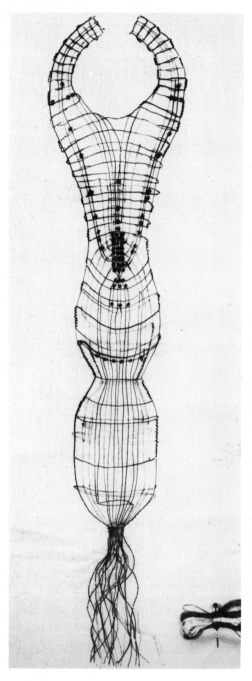

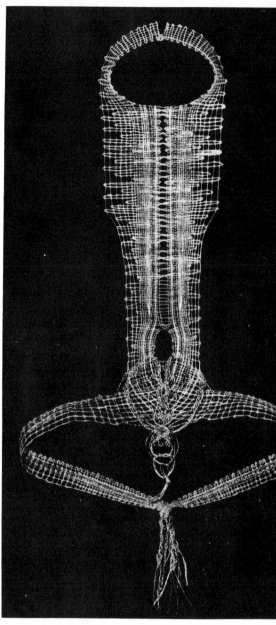

Fig. 86 Lace inner part; this is pushed through the lace in fig. 85 to produce the work shown in fig. 83

Fig. 87 Necklace combined with a belt to form a frontispiece, worked in natural thread with gold and silver, designed by Marie Vankova Kuchynkova

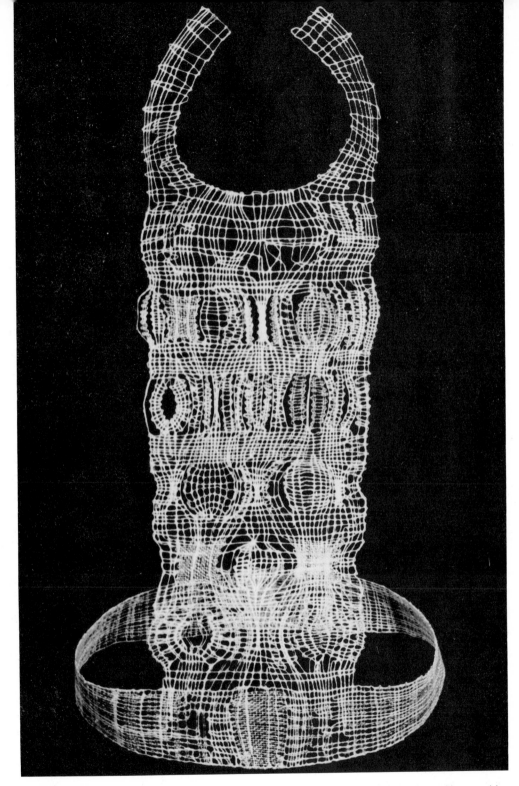

Fig. 88 Necklace and belt forming a wide frontispiece in black and gold worked and designed by Marie Vankova Kuchynkova.

This needs to be carefully shaped to mould the figure and would probably be worked on a figure shape or tailor's dummy

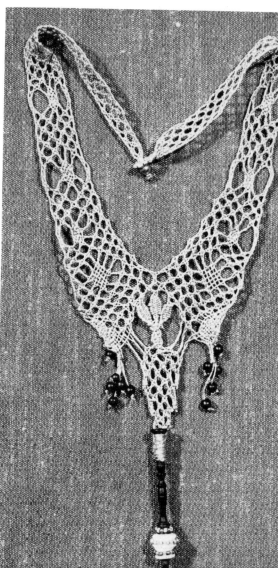

Fig. 89 LEFT Space lace flower in a shopping precinct designed and worked by Kaethe Kliot in dyed sisal, 2.9 × 2.13m (9ft 6in × 7ft)

Fig. 91 TOP RIGHT A rectangle of Torchon ground and spiders worked in coarse thread of a size to make a cushion cover. By Kaethe Kliot

Fig. 92 BOTTOM RIGHT Contemporary handkerchief edges made in Germany

Fig. 90 RIGHT Simple Torchon necklace in gold thread with an antique Danish bobbin incorporated in the design. By Kaethe Kliot

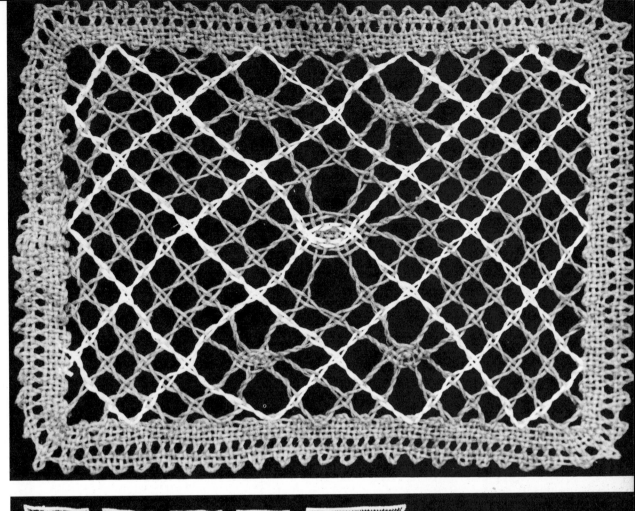

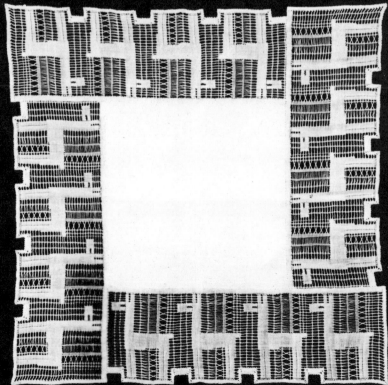

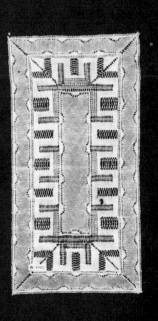

Fig. 93 ABOVE Contemporary lace insets designed and made at the Lace school in Nordhalben, Germany

Fig. 94 ABOVE Centre of a mat in tape lace showing the shaded effect of using graduated colours, light to dark. Made in the Lace school at Nordhalben, Germany

Fig. 95 BELOW Madonna design, by Martine Bruggeman, 43 × 50cm (17 × 20in)

Fig. 96 RIGHT Girl with Flowers, by Martine Bruggeman, 52 × 30cm (20½ × 12in)

Fig. 97 BELOW Flower panel, by Martine Bruggeman, 52 × 40cm (20½ × 16in). Martine is one of the leading designers in Bruges. She is an artist and helps with design at the Kantcentrum as well as designing for the Animated Work Group and producing some commercial designs for lace

Fig 98 Angel designed for the top of the Christmas tree worked from a paper shape (origami) and folded into position to give dimension. Stiffened with hair spray

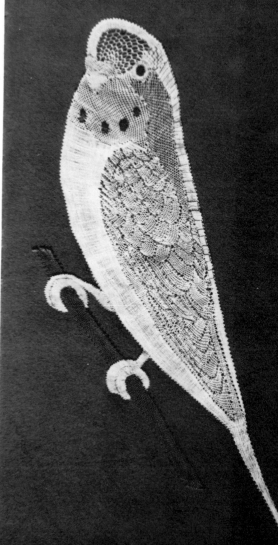

Fig. 99 Budgerigar designed and worked by Veronic Sorenson. 45 × 15cm (18 × 6in)

Fig. 100   Dimensional scene of a deer in a wood, worked in 1-ply wool in shades of green and fawn

Fig. 101   Birds in suspension in mauve and pink stranded cotton, Sylko perle and 1-ply wool. Two layers worked separately and attached to the box frame, one behind the other

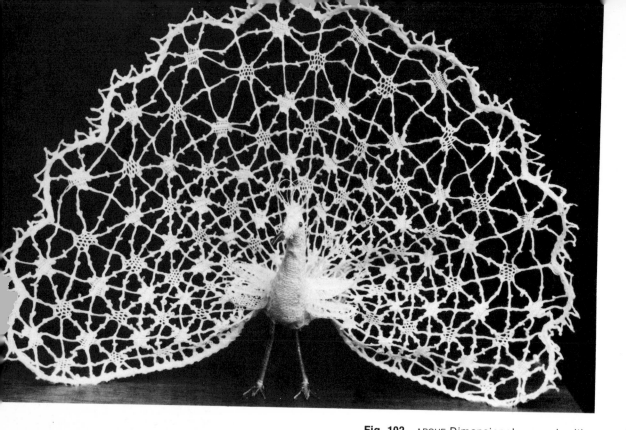

Fig. 102 ABOVE Dimensional peacock with a Bedfordshire lace tail, the body worked as in the dimensional cockered with wired legs and the tail planned as a half-circle. Millinery wire is used as the gimp on the outer tail to hold it in position

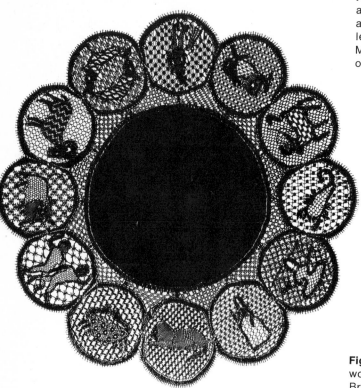

Fig. 103 LEFT Zodiac mat designed and worked as a sampler of stitches. By Bridget Cook

Fig. 104 Willow pattern motif worked in
Chantilly style in blue silk. Designed and
worked by Alexandra Stillwell. The use of
different stitches to break up the design
into parts has proved most effective

Fig. 105   The Rainbow, by Mme Valerie Paton of Brussels, 23 × 16cm (9 × 6in). Worked for the 1981 Brussels Miniature Textiles Exhibition, in cotton thread 50, with colours used for the rainbow

Sources of Design

Historical
Manuscript illuminations
Egyptian tomb paintings
Pottery decoration
Textile decoration
Oriental carpets
Cave paintings
Brass rubbings
Antique laces
Stained glass
Jacobean crewel embroidery
Blackwork embroidery
Cross stitch samplers
Folk art

Natural
Plants, leaves, grasses, flowers, ferns,
    trees, fruit, seed heads

Animals, insects, fish, birds
Seaweed, shells
Molecular structures
Reflections
Bark rubbings
Snowflakes, frost patterns
Leaf and fish skeletons

Others
Greetings cards
Magazine illustrations
Children's art
Wrought iron
Chinese paper cuts
Abstract oil on water patterns
Illustrated book covers
Wall paper

Lace Equipment Suppliers

UK
Audrey Sells
49 Pedley Lane
Clifton
Shefford
Bedfordshire

D.J. Hornsby
149 High Street
Burton Latimer
Kettering
Northants

Mace and Nairn
89 Crane Street
Salisbury
Wiltshire
SP1 2PY

Ken & Pat Schulz
Coppins
Ixworth Road
Honington
Bury St Edmunds
Suffolk
IP31 1QY

Frank Herring & Sons
27 High West Street
Dorchester
Dorset
DT1 1UP

E. Braggins & Sons
23–36 Silver Street
Bedford
Bedfordshire

All branches of John Lewis

Stephen Simpson
Avenham Road Works
Preston
Lancashire
(*gold and lurex threads*)

Jack Piper
Silver Lea
Flax Lane
Glemsford
Suffolk
(*silk threads*)

For information on all aspects of lace write to:

USA
Berga Ullman Inc
P.O. box 918
North Adams
Mass. 01247

Frederick J. Fawcett
129 South Street
Boston
Mass. 02130

Osma G. Tod Studio
319 Mendoza Avenue
Coral Gables
Florida 33134

Robin and Russ Handweavers
533 N. Adams Street
McMinnville
Oregon 97128

Lacis
2990 Adeline Street
Berkeley
California 94703

Belgium
Manufacture Belge de Dentelle
6 Galerie de la Reine
Galeries Royales St Hubert
1000 Bruxelles
Belgique

For information on all aspects of lace write to:

UK
The Lace Guild
High Gate
Newtown
Newbury
Berkshire

USA
International Old Lacers
P.O. Box 1029
Westminster
Colorado 80030

Belgium
Kantcentrum
Balstraat 14
8000 Brugge

France
Centre d'Initiation à la
    dentelle du Puy
2 rue Duguesclin
4300 Le Puy

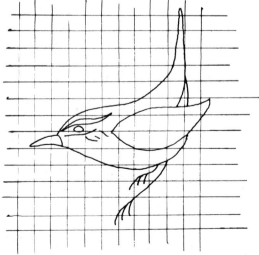

Diagram 105 How to enlarge or diminish
a drawing. Draw a grid over the drawing.
Make another grid to the size required, for
example twice or half the size of the
original, and draw in the same details
within the squares of the grid

136

Grids

The graph papers are useful for plotting regular grounds and fillings and are shown with some marked for different purposes and threads.

Diagram 106 millimetre paper

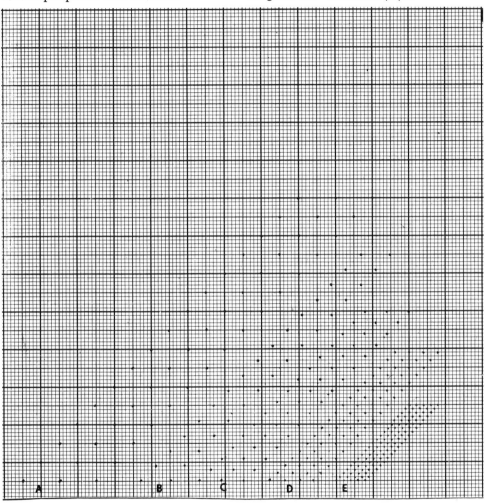

A For 1-ply wool, coton à broder, cordonnet 60 to 100, 35 linen, 40 to 60 crochet cotton, 3 to 6 strands Anchor stranded

B Close ground with threads from A, more open in 40 to 50 linen, 2 strands Anchor, DMC 20, Sylko 36, Coats Italian 30 and Fil à Dentelle

C Close ground with threads from B, more open with 50 linen, Sylko 40, Coats Italian 50 and DMC 30

D Close ground with threads from C, more open with 50 Sylko 1-strand Anchor, 90 to 100 linen and DMC 50

E 120 to 180 Honiton thread, 120 to 150 linen and DMC 60 to 100

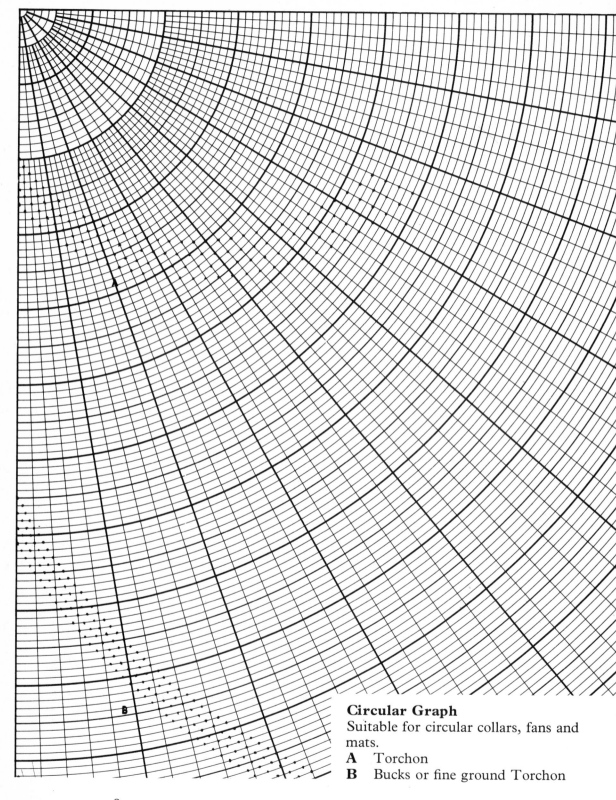

Circular Graph
Suitable for circular collars, fans and mats.
A   Torchon
B   Bucks or fine ground Torchon

Isometric Paper
For Bucks patterns.

Grounds Marked for Fillings

A Torchon, Lille, Rose ground and
 striped ground
B Honeycomb, Mayflower
C Brussells or Mechlin
D Torchon spider
E Snatch bar or Toad in the hole
F Lattice and cutwork

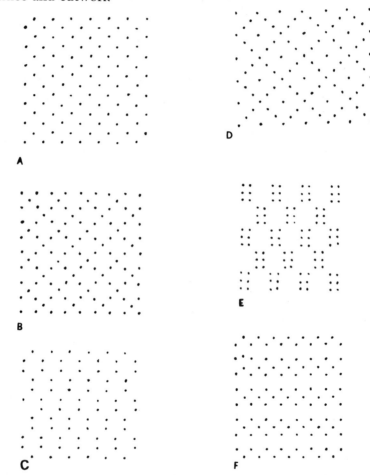

A

B

C

D

E

F

Useful Books for Inspiration

The Book of Bobbin Lace Stitches, Bridget Cook and Geraldine Stott
The Technique of Honiton Lace, Elsie Luxton
The Technique of Bobbin Lace, Pamela Nottingham
English Crewel Designs, Mary Eirwen Jones
The Courtship of Birds, Hilda Simon
Medieval Hunting Scenes, Gaston Phoebus
Pressed Flower Pictures and Collages, Pamela McDowall
A Field Guide to Insects, Dr Jiri Zahradnik
Greek Ornament, Edited by Patrick Connell
A Treasury of Design for Artists and Craftsmen, Gregory Mirow
Designs and Patterns for Embroiderers and Craftsmen, edited by Marion Nichols
Art Form in Nature, Ernst Haeckel
Art Forms from Plant Life, William M. Harlow
Geometric Design and Ornament, selected by Edmund V. Gillow Jr

Index